# ISLAND

# SALMON FISHERMAN

# ISLAND
# SALMON FISHERMAN

## by Robert H. Jones and Larry E. Stefanyk

HARBOUR PUBLISHING

Harbour Publishing Co. Ltd
P.O. Box 219, Madeira Park, BC V0N 2H0
www.harbourpublishing.com

Edited by Betty Keller
Text Design by Warren Clark
Printed in Canada
Cover photograph by Janice M. Stefanyk

Harbour Publishing acknowledges financial support from the Government of Canada through the Book Publishing Industry Development Program and the Canada Council for the Arts, and from the Province of British Columbia through the BC Arts Council and the Book Publishing Tax credit.

 **Canada Council for the Arts** **Conseil des Arts du Canada**

 BRITISH COLUMBIA ARTS COUNCIL Supported by the Province of British Columbia

**Library and Archives Canada Cataloguing in Publication**
Jones, Robert H., 1935-
    Island salmon fisherman : Vancouver Island Hotspots / Robert H. Jones and Larry E. Stefanyk.
Includes index.
ISBN 978-1-55017-425-0
    1. Pacific salmon fishing—British Columbia—Vancouver Island—Guidebooks. 2. Pacific salmon fishing—Equipment and supplies.
3. Vancouver Island (B.C.)—Guidebooks. I. Stefanyk, Larry E. II. Title.
SH686.J66 2008      799.17'56097112      C2008-900374-8

DISCLAIMER
There is no actual or implied warranty concerning the accuracy or suitability of the map coordinates listed in this book for any uses whatsoever. The authors, publisher, and sources of cartographic information expressly disclaim any responsibility for any loss or damage resulting from the use of these coordinates or related information.

# DEDICATION

To the memory of Corey David Hayes, one of the finest fishing guides who ever plied the waters off the coast of British Columbia. He made lasting friendships wherever he went before leaving us at the far too young age of 35 on November 11, 2007

# ACKNOWLEDGEMENTS

This "honour roll" is a list of those who provided us with in-depth interviews about their specific locales and shared their knowledge about the tackle and techniques that worked best for them, salmon run timing, typical weather patterns, peak fishing periods and so forth. Included are well-known fishing guides, resort operators, folks who work in the retail fishing tackle business, and a few tackle manufacturers. An impressive list, indeed. In alphabetical order they are Bruce Aikman (Aikman's Angling, Campbell River), Ian Andersen (Silver Fox Charters, Port Hardy), Bryon Armstrong (former owner Painter's Lodge, Campbell River), Mike Barker & Lynn Mooney (Kyuquot Beach House, Kyuquot Sound), Russ Bartrim (Vi-Dean Charters, Parksville), Dan Boudreau (Gone Fishin', Comox Valley), Dick Brune (Island Sun Charters, French Creek), Bruce Chard (Chinootka Lodge, Nootka Sound), Dick Close (former owner Weigh West Marine Resort, Tofino), Tom Davis (Rhys Davis Ltd., Sidney), Al Ehranberg (Gone Fishin', Port Alberni), Doug Ferguson (Coastline Salmon Charters, Bamfield), Doug Field (Buzz Bomb/Zzinger Lures, Courtenay), the late Dave Fletcher (Morning Sun Charters, Campbell River), Vern Friesen (Denverlene Charters, Comox), Murray Gardham (former owner Double Bay Fishing Resort, Blackfish Sound), Mark Grant (Mark Grant's Charters, Sooke), the late Corey Hayes (Corey's Fishing Charters, Port Hardy), Liz Hicks (former owner Tyee Resort, Bamfield), Ken Jenkins (Codfather Charters, Port Hardy), Pat Johnson, former owner Sealand Tackle, Nanaimo), Ed Jordan (Sutil Charters, Heriot Bay), Dan Kirby (Hidden Cove Lodge, Beaver Cove), Venz Kuzev (former owner Iris Lodge, Zeballos), Brian Lacroix (Brian Lacroix Salmon Charters, Sooke), Gail and Richard Leo (Swansong Marina, Fair Harbour), Jake Leyenaar (Jake's Charters, Port Alberni), David Manson (Megan Cruising, Campbell River), Bill Martin (Smoothy Charters, Parksville), Glen Massick (AGM Outdoorsman's Pit Stop, Parksville), Jason Mohl (Jay's Clayoquot Ventures, Tofino), Shawn Moore (former manager, Pedder Bay Marina, Victoria), Marilyn & David Murphy (Murphy Sportfishing, Port Alberni/Kyuquot Sound), Adrian O'Connor (Reel Obsession Sport Fishing, Zeballos), Dan O'Connor & Cristina Lepore (Mason's Lodge, Zeballos), Martin Paish (former Northern Operations Manager, Oak Bay Marine Group, Victoria), Skip & Susan Plensky (Sea Otter Lodge, Kyuquot Sound), Norm Reite (former owner Island West Resort, Ucluelet), Hans Schuer (Fishing Guide, Sayward), Bill Shire (Codfather Charters, Port Hardy), Ken Smith (Eagle Claw Charters, Port Hardy), Rod Sullivan (Saltwater Salmon Charters, Sooke), Brian Taylor (King Coho Resort, Comox), Del Thompson (manager, Schooner Cove Marina), Jeanne Usher (Breaker's Marine, Bamfield), Tom Vaida (Island Outfitters Sportfishing Centre, Victoria), Greg Vance (The Outpost at Winter Harbour), Robert Van Pelt (**Pacific Bait and Tackle**), Bill von Brendel (Just Fish'n, Ucluelet), Gordon Webb (Deep Bay Fishing Resort, Deep Bay), Murray Whelan (Tyee Marine, Campbell River), Elliot Williams (fishing guide, Port Renfrew), and Kim Zak (independent fishing guide).

# TABLE OF CONTENTS

# INTRODUCTION

M ost anglers have probably read or heard the statement that "10 percent of the fishermen catch 90 percent of the fish." Believe it. And believe also that the people who form this elite group never depend on "fisherman's luck." They have an intimate knowledge of their fishing tackle, their boat's navigational and electronic equipment, the water in which they fish, their quarry, and a range of proven techniques on which they can draw to meet virtually any situation that might ever be encountered while out on the water. The less fortunate 90 percent can usually attribute their consistent lack of success to some or all of the following:

- lack of knowledge about when and where to go fishing.
- inexperience at choosing and using lures or baits.
- inattention to details while out on the water.
- lack of knowledge about the proper use of a marine chart, compass, depth sounder, global positioning system and/or other boating and navigational equipment.
- unsuitable tackle for the task.

Larry Stefanyk and I hope that by reading this book you will learn where and when to go salmon fishing around Vancouver Island and also pick up pointers in other areas where you might require improvement or consider practising in order to become a more efficient angler.

*Island Fisherman* publisher Larry Stefanyk with a prime feeder chinook salmon.

*Island Fisherman* editor Bob Jones caught this 14-pound coho on a fly while fishing on Clayoquot Sound.

Those who have read *The Island Halibut Fisherman* will note some similarities to this book since geography, weather patterns, safety practices, and the historical background of the various destinations remain the same. When we started compiling it in 2006, Larry and I decided that, while we are experienced saltwater fishermen, we are not experts. As the publisher and editor respectively of *Island Fisherman* magazine, we meet many people who share our interest in recreational fishing, including professional fishing guides. During one active season they probably experience more time on the water than most anglers will in 10 years, so whenever possible we arrange to interview them. Some of their tales are humorous while others are harrowing, but all are interesting because guides are treasure troves of information, advice and useful tips.

Over the years some excellent books about saltwater salmon fishing have been written by British Columbian authors who are recognized experts in this field. Among those written in the 1970s and '80s that are still valuable sources of information are works by Charlie White, Alec Merriman, Jim Gilmore, Lee Straight, David Nuttall, Bruce Colgrave, Jack Gaunt and Mike Cramond. Some have been revised and remain in print, while others occasionally show up in second-hand bookstores and yard sales. All are well worth acquiring—and reading. A bibliography of them is included at the end of this book. In addition, a few books written by Vancouver Islanders have appeared more recently. In *Island Fly Fisherman,* Tim Tullis of Parksville details open water fly fishing for salmon, Frank Dalziel of Lantzville covers beach fishing for pinks and coho, Kevin Reid of Miracle Beach deals with beach fishing for sea-run cutthroat trout, and yours truly covers dredging flies for bottom fish. Another recent release from Harbour Publishing—*Maximum Salmon* by Dennis C. Reid—covers salmon fishing from Alaska to northern California.

# 1 FOR VISITORS TO VANCOUVER ISLAND

• • • • • • • • • • • • • • • • • • • • • • • •

Each year Vancouver Island's resident saltwater anglers are joined by thousands more from elsewhere in the world. Most are seeking Pacific salmon—usually chinooks for their size and strength and coho for their speed and acrobatic fight. However, there is more to salmon fishing than these two admittedly noble species because frisky pink and sockeye salmon provide excellent sport on light tackle, and large chum salmon are noted for their tough, tackle-punishing battles.

Anglers also target non-salmonids—collectively called "bottom fish"—some intentionally, as in the case of halibut, but mostly in combination with planned salmon trips. Most popular are Pacific halibut that generally range from 15 to 40 pounds but frequently tip the scales at 100 pounds or more. Lingcod have been recorded to 100 pounds, but these days most average between 5 and 30 pounds. Nevertheless, lingcod of 50-plus pounds are still fairly common in areas that are not heavily fished. There are also about two dozen species of rockfish, most prized of which are yelloweye rockfish for their large size and succulent flesh and black rockfish for the fast-paced surface action they provide to fly fishers and light tackle enthusiasts.

The saltwater fishing potential around Vancouver Island relates directly to its rugged, tortuous shoreline. Hundreds of

Bjorn Bostrom of Sweden caught this 44-pound chinook while fishing out of Sooke with guide Adrian O'Connor.
*Reel Obsession Sport Fishing photo*

sounds, inlets and bays are dotted with islands large and small, and between them meander multitudes of channels and passages, all creating marvellous structures for small aquatic creatures and the fish that feed on them. Flowing into the ocean from many of the islands are thousands of trickles, creeks and rivers, most of which yield anadromous fish, such as coastal cutthroat trout, Dolly Varden, steelhead, and runs that represent some or all five species of Pacific salmon: chinook, chum, coho, pink and sockeye.

Depending on the season and location, saltwater anglers on Vancouver Island who are so inclined may also fish freshwater streams and lakes for sea-run steelhead, cutthroat trout, Dolly Varden and kokanee, and some places also offer brown trout plus smallmouth and largemouth bass.

## Accommodations

While some popular fishing destinations are located in remote wilderness settings approachable only by boat or floatplane, every year trophy-sized salmon and halibut are also weighed in at marinas located in major cities like Victoria, Nanaimo and Campbell River. Happily, this situation is true as well at dozens of much smaller communities located all around the Island.

Pacific Safari Lodge is anchored in McBride Bay on Nootka Island.

The types and classes of accommodations available at these destinations vary enough to suit the desires and economics of everyone. Choices range from simply parking your camper or pitching a tent wherever the mood strikes, booking in at a rustic British Columbia Forest Service campground, or staying at fully serviced commercial campgrounds and RV parks right on up through various levels of bed and breakfast operations, motels and hotels (some of which offer fishing packages), to fishing lodges and resorts that range from meeting basic requirements to those catering to your every whim (when you are not out fishing, of course).

A few words of caution: if considering a holiday at such popular salmon fishing destinations as Port Alberni, Bamfield, Tofino, Campbell River and Port Hardy, to avoid disappointment it pays to book accommodations well in advance—meaning at least three months and longer if possible. Most repeat visitors make their arrangements one year ahead.

## Planning Your Fishing Vacation

The bottom line when planning a fishing vacation depends on three main factors: what you want to catch, how much time you have, and how much you can afford to spend.

BC Tourism has an excellent information package available for anglers interested in fishing the coastal waters. All you need to start planning a trip is to contact them at 1-800-663-6000 or 1-800-HELLO BC (435-5622) or visit their website at www.HelloBC.com. For specific information on saltwater and freshwater fishing, www.bcfishing.com provides the basics on what is available, licensing requirements, and links to the BC Fishing Resort Owners Association.

There are numerous road-accessible resorts plus several remote fishing lodges located on the North Island. While most cater to saltwater anglers, many also offer excellent freshwater fishing opportunities, and some even have access to golf courses and other forms of recreation. With the availability of web sites and information brochures, you can narrow the field by spending some time investigating precisely what each specific destination has to offer. For most diehard anglers the paramount point should be the fishing potential based on the average numbers that are caught or, if seeking trophy fish, the average of the largest sizes of your target species. Once you have winnowed out the destinations that don't stack up to your expectations, determine the following basic points:

- If the lodge is at a remote location, are connecting travel services provided?
- If air travel is involved, what is the maximum allowable luggage weight?
- Do meals include early and late breakfasts, boxed lunches, and snacks? If required, can they cater to special dietary needs? Are alcoholic beverages supplied or available for purchase?
- Is fishing tackle and rain clothing (including footwear in your size) provided? Are local lures and fly patterns available to purchase?
- Is cleaning, freezing, packaging and shipping of fish included?

Some operations offer guided and unguided packages. First-time visitors generally use guides, but repeat customers have often learned the areas and techniques well enough to fish unguided if they wish to. Ask the following questions:

- Is guided fishing provided as part of the package or does it cost extra?
- Are boats outfitted with marine charts, compasses, VHF radios, depth sounders, and Global Positioning Systems (GPS)?
- If you plan on fly fishing, are the boats suitable?

Information packages from reputable operations usually include recent catch statistics, pictures of guests with fish and a list of personal references. The latter can be an excellent source of information as nothing beats personal points of view and advice from people who have experienced one or more stays at a particular resort. The best indication of an operation's overall quality is the number of repeat visits regular guests make each year. Most avid anglers would rather stay at a rustic camp with limited services and good fishing than at a luxury resort with only modest fishing. However, it is possible to get the best of both worlds. In most cases, all it takes on your part is a bit of homework ahead of time.

Casting flies for Pacific salmon and bottom fish is increasing in popularity. It got its biggest boost here in Clayoquot Sound during the mid-1990s.

You may have a choice of three plans: American, housekeeping or outpost. While the level of accommodations, services and amenities might vary, the basic concept of each plan is as follows:

American plan: the best option for those wanting to maximize their time fishing, exploring, or simply relaxing. This plan provides accommodations, all meals, room service and amenities. Rates may be based on double occupancy, so check beforehand. Also determine whether or not fishing guides and/or the use of boats and motors are included in the package price.

Housekeeping plan: great for family vacations, small groups of friends and those on a budget. This plan includes accommodations—often in a cabin or cottage—furnishings, cooking facilities, utensils, dishes and cutlery but does not include food. Check beforehand whether or not bedding is provided.

Outpost plan: popular with couples or small groups interested in fishing at remote locations accessible only by floatplane, boat or four-wheel drive vehicle. Accommodations under this plan are often rustic, meaning a permanent tent camp or cabin with no running water or electricity, and provide only basic sleeping arrangements and cooking facility with utensils, dishes and cutlery. You supply your own food, bedding and fishing equipment. Boats, motors and fuel are usually supplied.

## Hiring a Fishing Guide

When fishing new waters, the best investment a visiting angler can make is to hire a reputable guide. Remember that neither age nor gender are criteria for being a good guide since those in their teens or early twenties may have been fishing since they were toddlers. Most resorts have guides available on a permanent or casual basis, and some guides have such enviable reputations that they are known in angling circles throughout the world.

If you have specific requirements, make them known as much in advance as possible. If, for example, you intend to fly fish, request a guide with similar interests so you can ask questions concerning fly patterns and casting techniques.

Although most guides conduct themselves in a businesslike, professional manner, personality conflicts do occur on occasion. If possible, try to spend some time speaking with a guide prior to making a commitment. This is especially important if his/her services will be required

Nootka Sound fishing guide David Chard holds up his happy customer's trophy-sized chinook.
*Chinootka Lodge photo*

for several days. Be very specific about what you hope to accomplish and how. Then, if there are any disagreements or any sense of discomfort or unease on the part of you or the guide, arrangements can be made to seek someone else.

# 2 GETTING AROUND VANCOUVER ISLAND BY ROAD

O n southern Vancouver Island, Highway 14 runs west from Victoria to Sooke, then 72 km to Port Renfrew. Destinations on the southern west coast of Vancouver Island—including Sooke, Jordan River and Port Renfrew—are all reached via Highway 14.

Highway 19/19A extends about 500 km northwest from Victoria to Port Hardy. The original route north, which includes the Oceanside Island Highway 19A, borders the eastern shoreline until well past Campbell River. This provides an interesting drive through several small, pleasant communities and towns, a few of which offer good fishing potential. However, drivers in a hurry to reach northern destinations can use the newer Inland Island Highway 19 from Victoria to

The major recreational fishing ports around Vancouver Island.

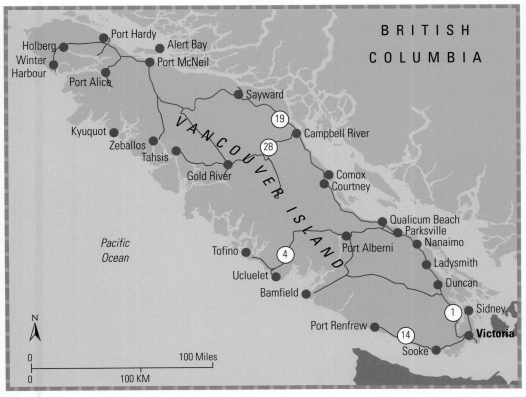

Campbell River. All west coast destinations on central and northern Vancouver Island are reached by branch roads from Highway 19/19A. These include Port Alberni, Bamfield, Ucluelet and Tofino, all via Highway 4; Gold River via Highway 28, which continues on to Tahsis by gravel road; Zeballos and Fair Harbour via gravel road; Port Alice and Coal Harbour by paved roads; and Holberg, Cape Scott Park and Winter Harbour via gravel roads.

Gravel roads and dry weather create uncomfortable driving conditions that can also have a detrimental effect on your boat, motor, and other equipment. If towing a boat, ensure that it has a tightly fitting cover to reduce the amount of dust that reaches its interior. Outboard motors should also be tightly covered. Do not carry fishing tackle in the boat or the back of a pickup truck unless it is in a dustproof container. Close the vehicle windows tightly and turn on the fan or air conditioner to its highest setting as the buildup of internal pressure will keep the dust at bay.

Much of the Island's west coast remains roadless, so getting to fishing lodges in these areas requires the use of aircraft or boats. This is also the case with a few lodges located in Blackfish Sound and Queen Charlotte Strait at the Island's northeastern end.

# PART TWO

# 3 ON THE WATER

## Fishing Regulations

The *British Columbia Tidal Waters Sport Fishing Guide*, produced by Fisheries and Oceans Canada, details everything you can and cannot do while fishing in saltwater. The coastal region is divided into 29 inshore and 9 offshore management areas. While general regulations and restrictions apply coast wide, some management areas may have site-specific restrictions or closures, spot closures during certain periods or adjusted size and possession limits. An integral part of this guide is the *British Columbia Freshwater Salmon Supplement*, which covers fishing regulations for salmon fishing in freshwater.

Before going fishing, ensure that you are properly licensed and tagged, and make it a point to become familiar with the regulations concerning size and possession limits. Pay particular attention to the regulation on preparing and wrapping fish prior to transporting your catch. It can save you a lot of grief—and money—should you be stopped at a road check.

## Understanding Tides

High-liners, the people who consistently catch more salmon than everyone else, usually know when to fish—and when not to. Virtually everything they do is planned around a well-thumbed regional tide guide because they know that major and minor feeding periods are directly linked to tidal flows as fish seek the areas where currents will supply them with food. In some cases, however, salmon may be present simply because there is enough water in which to move around and forage, as coho do when they feed in shallow, knee-deep water close to shore.

To appreciate the importance of tides, consider the fact that

This boat will remain beached until high tide.

## Tidal Terms

**Tide:** Refers to the alternate rising and falling of the sea twice each lunar day at a given point on earth, a movement that is caused by the attraction of the moon and sun. The moon creates the greatest attraction and the sun about half as much. As a result, water in oceans and lakes bulges outward from whichever portion of the earth is in direct line with the moon.

**Flood tide:** the current associated with a rising tide that moves toward shore and will push right up an estuary or river. Also called a rising, flooding or incoming tide.
**Ebb tide:** the current that moves away from shore, also called a falling tide.
**Slack tide:** the short interval at peak high or low tide periods when a tidal current stops, then changes direction.

salmon are opportunistic feeders and won't work any harder than they must for a meal. Some may race around herding and slashing through a ball of herring while others simply stay below the ball and wait for the dead and wounded baitfish to flutter down to them.

Baitfish find it easier to swim around in search of food during slack tides, so this is when they often move close to the surface. In fast-running tides they relocate to the bottom where there is less current speed due to the "boundary layer effect." Slow and slack water periods, therefore, usually offer the best fishing opportunities, but between the extremes of slack and fast-running currents baitfish and the salmon following them will be on the move at various depths. Determine where these depths are and your chances for hook-ups will improve accordingly.

When trolling, you will often have strikes while travelling in one direction but nothing on the return tack. In all likelihood you are trolling with the current one way and against it on the other. Salmon face into the current, so when you are travelling upstream, you are presenting your bait from behind them, which is unnatural. Determine which way the tide is flowing and then troll at an angle across the current, which provides salmon with a wider range of vision.

When salmon (and bottom fish) are feeding, they often rest downstream from a structure that breaks the current—a kelp bed, shoal, island, pinnacle, rock pile, or point of

Fish normally face into the current, so troll or cast in front of a moving school.

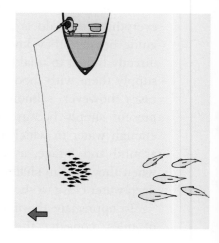

land—where they can leisurely await the arrival of food washing downstream toward them.

Estuaries are natural feeding stations and salmon usually continue feeding there until a freshet raises water levels in the stream. Schools are usually found there during any tide level, with the main variable being their distance from shore. Vary your search pattern accordingly, and especially try the outer edges of drop-offs on falling ebb (best) or early flood tides.

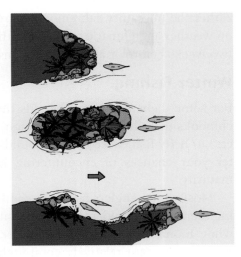

Fish often use a structure to break the current while holding in position, waiting for food to wash toward them.

## Periods of Abundance

Depending on the time of year, the most productive areas for salmon are major feeding grounds, spawning migration routes and the estuaries of their natal rivers, especially those with successful salmon hatcheries. A typical feeding ground has ample year-round forage like herring, anchovies, needlefish, pilchards, krill, shrimp and squid. They are good bets for immature feeder chinooks, which, depending on their age, might range in size from smolts to fish weighing up to 30 pounds.

During winter months, juvenile coho are found in areas with large populations of euphausiid shrimp (*Euphausia pacifica*), the most common North Pacific species of krill, but during late spring or early summer they switch to eating baitfish and start gaining size and weight at a truly amazing rate. Fish weighing only a pound or two in early spring might well be 15 pounds or more by September. Migratory northern coho, thought to be offshore ocean feeders, usually arrive from late summer to early autumn and average somewhat larger than the inshore stocks. However, some northern coho runs appear as late as December to early January.

As the other three Pacific salmon species are offshore feeders throughout the saltwater phase of their lives, they remain inaccessible to anglers until moving inshore on spawning migrations to their home rivers. Generally, the farther north you go on Vancouver Island the earlier the migratory salmon will start appearing. However, depending on weather and climatic conditions, there might be variations of one or two weeks before or after what is considered the "normal" run period.

## Winter Fishing

For some diehards, winter heralds the start of fishing for local feeder chinooks that, depending on location, will range from sub-legal "shakers" to hefty fish exceeding 30 pounds. The later in the season the better your chances of encountering larger fish that are approaching maturity.

Most winter anglers fish from comfortable day cruisers, simply placing their rods in holders while they sit in the cabin, sipping hot drinks while monitoring the depth sounder. Even those fishing from open boats can remain relatively comfortable thanks to a range of modern clothing that includes insulated jackets, trousers, footwear and gloves.

## Dealing with Seals

As harbour seal populations continue expanding along the entire West Coast, incidents of hooked salmon being intercepted and taken from anglers are increasing. The seals' response appears to be triggered by the sound of reel ratchets chattering as a hooked fish takes the line or by the sight of an angler fighting a salmon. While a healthy, free-swimming salmon can outswim a seal, these critters have learned that hooked salmon are easy pickings and they make the most of it. In some areas it is virtually impossible to land a salmon, so these areas are best avoided. When a seal grabs your salmon, keep a tight line on it as your partner runs the boat over top of the seal until your line is at an angle of about 10 to 20 degrees, then throttle back to the same speed as the seal is swimming. If you feel the line start to slack, it may indicate that the seal is surfacing for air, so adjust the boat's speed until your line is almost vertical in the water. Maintain pressure and make ready to net the salmon if and when the seal surfaces beside the boat. Your chances of retrieving your catch are slim, but this is the only method that works at least part of the time.

On occasion, sea lions and orcas will also take hooked salmon. Because of their size, they pose a threat of damage to the boat or propeller, so anglers should simply accept the loss.

# 4 CARING FOR YOUR CATCH

*U*nfortunately, after catching a fish many anglers simply toss it into an open container or on the deck where it quickly dries out, starts to rot and takes on a permanent curve. However, taking proper care of your catch guarantees that it will reach your table in prime condition and peak taste.

A limit of chinooks and coho waiting to be processed.

## Containers and Coolers

If a poll were taken to determine the most popular fish container used in small boats, plastic baby bathtubs would probably win. They are fine for short-term storage (and for bleeding fish), but only if the fish are covered to keep them cool and prevent drying out. A couple of burlap sacks or old terrycloth towels will do the job. Wet them down occasionally and then wring them partially dry. The moist cloth protects the fish from direct sunlight and evaporation keeps them fairly cool. If fishing close to a kelp bed, fresh kelp fronds can be laid over the fish to protect them. Any cover is better than nothing, but it must be kept damp at all times.

Some anglers use lightweight Styrofoam containers but few of these containers are sturdy enough to withstand much physical abuse. Placing the cooler inside a simple plywood box remedies the situation. The lid of the box, either hinged or removable, may also serve as a handy surface for cutting bait and cleaning fish.

Insulated coolers are available on the market in a wide range of sizes and styles, so it's simply a matter of choosing the largest that your boat

For prime eating, a catch is quickly cleaned and iced.

can accommodate comfortably. It should have a carrying handle at each end and a drainage hole at the bottom. Ideally, your cooler should be long enough to allow fish to be laid out straight. Trying to clean a fish that is bent like a pretzel by rigor mortis—the stiffening of muscle tissue after death—is difficult, and straightening it out tears the flesh apart.

## Cooling Your Catch

Among fishermen one school of thought says that if fish are kept cool for a few hours before cleaning and filleting, there is no need for ice. There are three caveats to this: the mean temperature, the length of time involved and the type of storage container. Fish stored for four or five hours inside of an in-hull compartment are usually still damp and cool to the touch when removed, even during hot weather conditions. Unfortunately, the same can't be said for fish contained in a portable cooler without ice during hot weather, not even for short periods.

Ice is the most efficient way to guarantee fresh fish. Some folks freeze water in cardboard milk cartons, but they inevitably leak as they defrost, and the water that collects in the bottom of the cooler soaks into the dead fish. Placing the cartons inside sealed plastic bags helps, but not if spiny-rayed species like rockfish go into the cooler. Reusable, gel-filled freezer packs are the answer. They are sturdy enough to resist punctures or cuts and stay frozen longer than plain ice.

Slime and blood also accumulate in the bottom of a cooler, and fish that soak in it are difficult to hang onto while handling and cleaning. A one-inch-high grid of wood, plastic or metal placed in the cooler's bottom will allow fluids to drain through, but you will need to drain the accumulated water and blood periodically.

## Killing and Bleeding a Salmon

Bonkers made by Dan Siminiuk.

Once you decide to keep a fish, kill it as quickly and humanely as possible, bleed it, keep it cool from the outset, and clean or fillet it as soon as time permits.

The most common method of killing a salmon is to hit it on top of the head with a club. This is quick and efficient. One hard, well-aimed blow will do, but two will confirm the job. Avoid swinging haphazardly at a fish suspended in a net, beating it about the sides or shoulder area. This won't deliver a killing blow and will bruise and discolour the flesh, making it much less eye-appealing.

Bleeding a salmon immediately after it is killed improves the colour and quality of its flesh.

After killing a salmon, grip its eye sockets firmly between the thumb and forefinger of your left hand (assuming right-handedness) and hold the fish over the gunwale. Use a sharp knife to cut behind the gill arches, following the curve of the bony gill collar, in order to sever the heart and ventral aorta. Then while still gripping the head with your left hand, grasp the wrist of the tail with your right hand and lift the fish straight up so that it is suspended head down. A surprising amount of blood will gush out quickly. After a few more seconds of final draining the fish may be placed in the cooler. This treatment improves the meat colour and quality but does not preclude cleaning or filleting the fish as soon as time permits.

Bleeding a large salmon is best done by two people—one holding the fish, the other wielding the knife. Rather than gripping the fish by its eye sockets, use a glove or piece of cloth to grasp the lower jaw or simply slip the point of a gaff hook into the fish's mouth and pull it out through a cheek or the lower jaw.

## Knives

Your tackle box should contain two knives: a sharp "general duty" knife for cutting bait, bleeding and cleaning fish and a filleting knife used specifically for that purpose. The cutting edge of a filleting knife blade should be sharpened at a shallow angle of about 10 degrees, which actually weakens the edge and makes it unsuitable for hacking at anything harder than skin or flesh. The edge of a general purpose knife blade should be sharpened at the more acute angle of about 20 degrees, which is sharp enough for most cutting jobs but can stand the abuse of cutting through the spine of a large fish.

A general purpose knife blade is much sturdier than that of a filleting knife's flexible blade.

The two most common filleting knife blade shapes are needle and scimitar.

The two most popular blade styles for filleting knives are scimitar—slightly curved and tapering to a slender point—and needle—a fairly straight blade of uniform depth throughout its length that curves upward into a point. Neither design has any real advantage over the other, so it's a matter of choice.

A cheap knife might appear equal to one costing much more, but the blade won't be of high-quality steel. You get what you pay for. Keep the blade razor-sharp. A keen cutting edge slices easily through skin and flesh with little pressure; a dull one requires more force combined with a sawing motion, and this often leads to accidents. Never abuse your filleting knife by cutting through bones or other hard material. When the knife is not in use, protect the blade by replacing it in its sheath.

Knife blades will dull from use so your tackle box should also contain a large carborundum stone or ceramic sharpening rods for touching them up as required.

A single filleting glove is recommended as it will make handling fish much easier and protect your hand from cuts. Filleting gloves are especially good for processing members of the rockfish family, which have sharp ridges on their head and gill covers; however, the glove will not provide protection from the needle-sharp spines of the dorsal, pelvic and anal fins.

# Cleaning a Salmon

**1.** Cut through the throat at the bottom of the gill collar.

**2.** Cut through the gills and then in front of the gill collar to the spine, severing the throat.

**3.** Cut through the spine behind the head.

**4.** Remove the head. (That's the heart dangling in front.)

**5.** Insert the knifepoint in the anus and cut forward up the belly.

**6.** Cut between the ventral fins and stop an inch or so behind the gill collar.

**7.** Cut around the inside of the gill cover to sever the gullet and throat.

**8.** After removing the guts, run the knifepoint down the centre of the kidney.

**9.** Use the spoon-shaped scraper on the knife handle to remove as much of the kidney as possible. If the knife lacks a scraper, use a discarded soup spoon or something similar.

**10.** Now is a good time to inspect the stomach contents to see what the salmon had been feeding on.

**11.** After washing off any blood, dirt or slime, place the salmon in a clean plastic bag. If you are using an endless tube, tie off one end with an overhand knot before cutting the tube to length.

**12.** Place the bagged salmon in a tub of water to expel all air.

**13.** Knot the top end of the tube tightly.

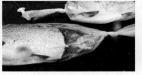

**14.** The salmon is now cleaned and bagged and ready for travel.

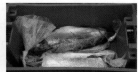

(Larger salmon may be cut into shorter lengths but the pieces must all travel together.)

## Filleting a Salmon

**1.** Insert the knifepoint into the anus and cut forward up the belly to the throat.

**2.** Cut close behind the gill collar to the spine.

**3.** Cut down the back with the knife blade riding on top of the dorsal bones.

**4.** Lift the fillet slightly and cut from front to rear, carefully flaying the flesh from the dorsal bones and spine.

**5.** Continue cutting carefully down toward the belly with the knife blade riding on top of the rib bones.

**6.** If you do not wish the belly meat on the fillet, you may turn the blade and trim it off from front to rear.

**7.** Flip the fish over and cut behind the gill collar to the spine. Repeat steps 3, 4, 5 and 6.

**8.** If you did not remove the belly meat while filleting, you may do so now.

**9.** Save the belly strips for bottom fishing—they make excellent halibut bait.

## Transporting Your Catch

The *British Columbia Tidal Waters Sport Fishing Guide* is quite specific about transporting and packaging fish. If you are stopped and checked by DFO enforcement officers, they must be able to identify the species, size and number of fish in your possession. This means leaving intact, with heads and tails on, all salmon that are of barely legal lengths and all barely legal lingcod in areas 11 to 21. This is fair because, with its head and/or tail removed, it is impossible to determine whether a fish was actually of the legal minimum size before cleaning. The regulations also state: "Where a fish has been filleted, the two whole fillets are considered as one fish, and the skin must not be removed from the fillet." In any case, the skin should always be left on salmon that are destined for barbecuing, baking or smoking. Be warned, however, that leaving the skin on fillets can reduce their eating quality unless a few simple precautions are taken while packaging them. Fish bodies are covered with a coating of slime that reduces friction as the fish move through the water and protects them from attack by parasites and disease organisms. However, if a fillet is stored with its outer skin side against the flesh side of another fillet, this slime will discolour the flesh and it will develop a strong, fishy odour.

Paul Gianera with salmon that was properly processed and packaged to permit easy identification while en route to his home in California.

# 5 PART THREE
# FISHING DESTINATIONS, ACCOMMODATION AND MARINE CHART COORDINATES

● ● ● ● ● ● ● ● ● ● ● ● ● ● ● ● ● ● ● ● ● ● ● ● ● ● ● ●

*C*oordinates listed in the Marine Charts sections are intended only for reference and planning purposes. All were calculated by the authors and are believed to be correct, but none of them should ever be used for navigation purposes until validated by cross-checking on the specific marine chart indicated. You, as the user, must assume full responsibility for determining the accuracy of any coordinates listed. Prior to making any critical navigational decision you must consult official sources, including marine charts and the monthly "Notices to Mariners."

Most place names following each destination section are taken from the *Gazetteer of Canada–British Columbia.* In cases where a name does not appear in the *Gazetteer* or is a local name, coordinates have been taken from the specific marine charts. Local names are shown within quotation marks to indicate that they do not appear on charts.

Read the latitudes northward from bottom to top of the chart and longitudes westward from right to left. Do not consider the coordinates

as "hotspots" but rather as locations to help you get around specific areas in order to eventually locate those hotspots. While programming a coordinate into your GPS beforehand will put you in "the ballpark," the waypoint for a specific hotspot should always be programmed on site for best results in relocating it.

Rupert Inlet in Quatsino Sound.

Depths on Canadian marine charts are indicated in metric. To convert metres to feet, simply multiply the metric number by 3.28 and print this number in the appropriate spot on the chart.

# Quatsino Sound

Queen Charlotte Strait is justifiably famous for its abundance of salmon and bottom fish. Unfortunately, it is also notorious for northwesters that can build quickly to 80 km/h producing unbelievably rough water conditions, and for frequent southeasters between mid-October and May that might blow for several days without dropping below 50 km/h. Whatever the time of year, whenever weather conditions refuse to cooperate with their fishing plans, Port Hardy anglers have an ace-in-the-hole called Quatsino Sound. It's simply a matter of trailering their boats to nearby Coal Harbour to launch them.

The most northerly of the five major sounds on the west coast of Vancouver Island, Quatsino cleaves northeast from Cliffe Point for 30

**Our Information Sources**

Ken Jenkins, owner, Codfather Charters, Port Hardy
Ken Smith, owner, Eagle Claw Charters, Port Hardy
Greg Vance, owner, The Outpost at Winter Harbour

**For visitor information:**

PORT HARDY VISITOR CENTRE
7250 Market Street
Box 249
Port Hardy, BC V0N 2P0
(250) 949-7622
phcc@cablerocket.com
www.ph-chamber.bc.ca

km. Near the entrance to Quatsino Narrows, Neroutsos Inlet swings southeast for 20 km past Jeune Landing, Port Alice, and the huge Neucel Specialty Cellulose pulp mill. Beyond Quatsino Narrows, Rupert Inlet continues northeast for 10 km past what was once the third largest copper mine in Canada, the open pit Island Copper Mine, a truly massive hole in the ground that is now flooded. Holberg Inlet cuts almost 35 km west to the community of Holberg, at one time the site of the world's largest floating logging camp and later a Royal Canadian Air Force radar station, part of the North American Air Defence (NORAD) system. The combined length of this roughly X-shaped network of water totals about 100 km, but being surrounded by steep mountains, it is fairly well protected from offshore winds.

The closest road access to Quatsino Sound is via the small community of Coal Harbour that is about 16 km west of Port Hardy. It was an RCAF seaplane base during the Second World War, then served as a whaling station from 1948 until the mid-1960s. Coal Harbour is now primarily a docking and fuelling area for commercial fishing vessels, logging company tugs and crew boats and for service boats for local aquaculture operations.

A private launch ramp and parking lot are located right beside the old seaplane hangar, which now houses the Air Cab office where you pay for launching. The wide gravel ramp has a moderate pitch so launching large boats is best accomplished at the top half of high tide. Space is limited at the private wharf, and the small government wharf is usually filled to capacity with commercial fishing boats.

Quatsino Sound is also accessible by gravel roads from Port Hardy. This involves driving 42 km west to Holberg, from where you can either drive 33 km southeast to Koprino Harbour or 25 km south to Winter Harbour. Note that these are active logging roads. At Koprino Harbour, about midway between Quatsino Narrows and the mouth of Quatsino Sound, the Spencer Cove Recreation Site is co-managed by the **Ministry of Tourism, Sports and the Arts** and Western Forest Products. It has a ramp suitable for small boats, a docking area, and 11 campsites.

Near the mouth of Quatsino Sound, Forward Inlet tucks in behind Cape Parkins and curves northward into the well-protected waters of Winter Harbour. This most western community in North America has a unique network of wooden boardwalks that connect the houses and buildings located along its shoreline—a reminder of the time prior to the 1970s when it was accessible only by boat or floatplane. At one time most of the community's economy was tied to commercial fishing and forestry but tourism now plays an increasingly important role. Among the accommodations available here for those interested in recreational fishing and nature tours are Dick's Last Resort, which also has cabins; Frosty's Winter Harbour with 2 floating cabins; Qualicum Rivers Fishing Resort, a full-service lodge overlooking the bay; and The Outpost at Winter Harbour with 35 RV sites, a boat launch, moorage, a full-service marina and a well-stocked general store. The latter two operations offer fishing packages with experienced, fully equipped guides. The 12-site Kwaksista Campground, operated by the District of Mount Waddington, is located about 1 km north of the community. The nearby boat launch is best used at high tide.

Boats of 14 to 16 feet are suitable for fair weather fishing within the confines of Quatsino Sound and the inlets, but for venturing offshore where high swells and choppy condi-tions are common, think in terms of larger and fully equipped craft with navigational aids.

## Weather and Water Conditions

Summer temperatures here average slightly cooler than southern Van-couver Island but are a bit warmer during the winter. Although the North Island annual rainfall averages 100 to 115 inches, Quatsino Sound is in a rain shadow so is somewhat drier. Nevertheless, appropriate wet

Janice Stefanyk with a tyee-class chinook.

weather clothing is always recommended. Most heavy rains occur from November through February, but there are occasional stretches of mod-erate, dry weather during the winter.

May or June can be unsettled with offshore westerlies blowing about 25 km/h; during summer highs occasional storm-force winds are south-easters, and these can be quite nasty.

Fog is relatively rare around Coal Harbour and Quatsino Narrows during the winter months. However, during warm weather conditions expect fog out near the mouth where it faces the open Pacific.

## Run Timing

Water temperature appears to play an important role in the timing of migratory salmon runs, so they occasionally vary rather dramatically. Shortly after the annual herring spawn, usually from late March to early April, a few of the first migratory "Columbia" chinooks start showing, and if there is a high pressure weather system, the local feeder chinooks go on a feeding binge. The chinook runs continue building and by late June and July coho and pinks will have joined them to feed actively around the mouth of Quatsino Sound, with Kains Island one of the most productive areas.

There are 3 rivers and 47 creeks emptying into Quatsino Sound and its adjoining inlets, and most of those that have not been disturbed by logging have small runs of coho. A hatchery on Stephens Creek near Coal Harbour produces a fair number of fish, and another run homes in on Waukwaas Creek near the top of Rupert Inlet. Some coho also head up Holberg Inlet into Hathaway Creek and the Goodspeed River. Immature coho (bluebacks) appear in the inlet in late March, April and May, and some late-running northern coho appear inside well into October.

There are chinooks in Quatsino Sound all year round, but throughout August and September a chinook closure inside Cliffe Point protects the Marble River run. However, traditionally there are still a few Marble River chinooks available after the closure ends on September 30, and a few can also be found migrating southward past the mouth of Quatsino Sound.

## Hotspots and Tactics

Ken Jenkins has fished Quatsino Sound off and on since 1986, mostly in the winter for feeder chinooks. He's usually busy guiding out of Port Hardy during the summer, but if the weather gets too rough, he simply trailers a boat over to Coal Harbour and gives his customers a change of scenery. He reports that in a boat cruising at 40 km/h it's about 45 minutes

Bruce Dirom, owner of Hardy Buoys Smoked Fish in Port Hardy, landed this prime 30-pound chinook while fishing in Quatsino Sound.

from Coal Harbour to Cliffe Point and another 15 minutes out to Kains Island. There is a good feeder chinook fishery from early December until early April, but with so much water and so few anglers only a few of the more popular locations receive any noticeable fishing pressure while many other potential hotspots are ignored.

Ken Jenkins' frequent winter fishing partner is Ken Smith, who also guides for Codfather Charters at Port Hardy. He says that the feeder chinooks they target range in size from sub-legal to a very respectable 30 pounds. Most of the early keepers weigh from 8 pounds up to the high teens, but they are somewhat larger by the end of March. They tend to stay deep because that is where the baitfish are found. On a slack tide they might occasionally be located between 30 and 60 feet but are usually below 60 feet.

As elsewhere, successful chinook fishing here relates directly to the tides. Big tides are nowhere near as productive as small ones, and slack periods are best. The standard winter tactic is downrigging with a flasher and hoochie—black/white, green/white, orange and red. Since the introduction of fluorescent and glow colours and of patterns such as purple haze, jellyfish, watermelon, Halloween and so forth, it's best to ask beforehand to determine what might be the hoochie du jour.

Depending on the time of year and variables such as weather, light conditions and bait availability, most winter fishing is concentrated around Quatsino Narrows, the northeastern side of Drake Island and in Neroutsos Inlet around the log dump at Jeune Landing. Between Quatsino Narrows and Drake Island there is a shelf at 24 metres across from the old log dump in Hecate Cove. Try downrigging back and forth along this shelf close to the bottom.

Once the migratory fish move in, most fishing pressure moves out to the mouth and offshore. According to Greg Vance of The Outpost at Winter Harbour, the most consistently productive early season setup is an Angelo's Green Gator or Yamashita 84M hoochie behind a standard Hot Spot green/silver flasher trolled reasonably fast at depths of 150 to 185 feet.

By late June and July, coho and pinks will have joined the chinooks around the mouth of Quatsino Sound, with Kains Island one of the

The "must have" hoochie in every angler's tackle box—green and white.

most productive areas. Mooching with cut-plug herring and drift-jigging are popular tactics with some anglers, but downrigging with a Tomic plug or a flasher and spoon is more effective, and trailing an anchovy or cut-plug herring behind a flasher on a 5- or 6-foot-long leader is most productive of all.

When the water temperatures are favourably cool in July and August—11° to 13°C (52°-56°F)—massive schools of herring and needlefish swarm into the nearshore waters from Brooks Peninsula to Cape Scott until the water is virtually boiling with baitfish. Most chinook and coho are taken at this time anywhere from the surface down to 120 feet, and there are ample opportunities for mooching, drift-jigging, bucktailing and fly fishing.

If an El Niño event warms water temperatures to 15°C (60°F), the salmon move offshore into deeper, cooler water. These events also see increased numbers of Pacific mackerel, which can be maddeningly annoying while fishing for salmon but lots of fun on fly-fishing tackle. (Hey, make the best of a bad situation!) This warm current also increases your chances of spotting a gigantic ocean sunfish basking on the surface or of hooking a blue shark.

When the August–September chinook closure is in effect, most fishing effort is just outside the Cliffe Point boundary, but you can also fish all the way down the beach for almost 2 km. There are usually coho and chinook farther out, but most effort will be centred on the sheltered waters behind Kains Island and the entrance to Forward Inlet. This area remains a hotspot from June to September, with the peak from about mid-July until mid-August. Migratory chinook heading for the Marble River are usually present until early September.

Trolling with plugs accounts for a lot of the coho caught in the Quatsino Sound area.

Anglers with fast, seaworthy boats can also explore farther offshore. If there is no westerly blowing and you can get around Cape Parkins, stay out beyond the surf line and head up into Grant Bay. This area receives heavy fishing pressure during the summer but is virtually impossible to fish in the winter because of southeasters and westerlies. Some good action can often be found about 4 km offshore from Kains Island in roughly 90 metres of water, where chinooks usually suspend at 120 to 150 feet. A good setup is a glow green Gatorback, purple haze or cotton candy hoochie behind a Hot Spot golden warrior flasher.

Coho are seldom plentiful deep inside Quatsino Sound during the summer though Cliffe Point and Koskimo Bay can be good. To the south, Restless Bight and Kwakiutl Point are productive, but getting there means venturing out onto the open water. About mid-August to early September when coho start moving toward their home streams, fishing picks up inside the inlets. Good bets then are Cliffe Point, Koskimo Bay, Koprino Harbour and Quatsino Narrows. The mouth of Stephens Creek near Coal Harbour also produces good coho fishing.

## AVAILABLE MARINE CHARTS

3617 Quatsino Sound
3681 Plans—Quatsino Sound: Coal Harbour, Quatsino Narrows, Neroutsos Inlet, Port Alice

## Marine Chart Coordinates:

| Place Names: | | Place Names: | |
| --- | --- | --- | --- |
| Brooks Peninsula | LAT 50°10' LONG 127°45' | Koskimo Bay | LAT 50°28' LONG 127°53' |
| Brown Rock | LAT 50°27' LONG 127°59' | Kultus Cove | LAT 50°29' LONG 127°37' |
| Cape Parkins | LAT 50°27' LONG 128°03' | Kwakiutl Point | LAT 50°21' LONG 127°59' |
| Cape Scott | LAT 50°47' LONG 128°26' | Mahatta River | LAT 50°28' LONG 127°48' |
| Cliffe Point | LAT 50°28' LONG 128°56' | Marble River | LAT 50°32' LONG 127°31' |
| Coal Harbour | LAT 50°36' LONG 127°35' | McAllister Islet | LAT 50°28' LONG 127°59' |
| Drake Island | LAT 50°30' LONG 127°40' | Monday Rocks | LAT 50°29' LONG 127°53' |
| Forward Inlet | LAT 50°30' LONG 128°02' | Neroutsos Inlet | LAT 50°24' LONG 127°31' |
| Gillam Islands | LAT 50°27' LONG 127°58' | Port Alice | LAT 50°23' LONG 127°27' |
| Gooding Cove | LAT 50°24' LONG 127°57' | Quatsino Narrows | LAT 50°33' LONG 127°34' |
| Goodspeed River | LAT 50°39' LONG 128°01' | Quatsino Sound | LAT 50°30' LONG 127°35' |
| Grant Bay | LAT 50°28' LONG 128°05' | Restless Bight | LAT 50°22' LONG 127°58' |
| Harvey Cove | LAT 50°26' LONG 127°55' | Robson Rock | LAT 50°26' LONG 128°01' |
| Hathaway Creek | LAT 50°35' LONG 127°46' | Rowley Reefs | LAT 50°24' LONG 127°58' |
| Hecate Cove | LAT 50°33' LONG 127°36' | Rupert Inlet | LAT 50°35' LONG 127°30' |
| Holberg | LAT 50°39' LONG 128°01' | South Danger Rock | LAT 50°26' LONG 128°00' |
| Holberg Inlet | LAT 50°36' LONG 127°44' | Spencer Cove Recreation Site | LAT 50°30' LONG 127°52' |
| Jeune Landing | LAT 50°26' LONG 127°29' | Stephens Creek | LAT 50°36' LONG 127°34' |
| Kains Island | LAT 50°27' LONG 128°02' | Waukwaas Creek | LAT 50°35' LONG 127°25' |
| Koprino Harbour | LAT 50°30' LONG 127°51' | Winter Harbour | LAT 50°32' LONG 128°00' |

The historical village of Zeballos is surrounded by towering mountains.

# Zeballos

The west coast of Vancouver Island attracts tens of thousands of salt-water anglers annually and this often results in crowded fishing conditions at the more popular locations. However, one with an excellent catch record that remains relatively uncrowded is Zeballos. How much longer this will continue remains to be seen because the area has been gaining a reputation for trophy-sized chinooks and coho.

The turnoff from Highway 19 to Zeballos and Fair Harbour is about 20 km northwest of Woss. There are plenty of hills on this 42-km stretch of winding gravel road and, as all of them have washboard surfaces, it pays to keep your speed down. It is an active logging road so you must remain constantly alert to oncoming traffic.

Although Zeballos receives thousands of visitors every summer, most are nature lovers, outdoor enthusiasts, ocean kayakers or people who are simply interested in the village's history. The number of saltwater and freshwater anglers has been fairly small but it is growing.

## Our Information Sources

Venz Kuzev, former owner, Iris Lodge
Adrian O'Connor, owner, Reel Obsession Sport Fishing
Cristina Lepore, co-owner, Zeballos Expeditions
Dan O'Connor, co-owner, Zeballos Expeditions

## For visitor information:

ZEBALLOS VISITOR CENTRE
Box 127
Zeballos, BC V0P 2A0
(250) 761-4070
www.zeballos.com

The community's name honours Ciriaco Cevallos, a lieutenant on one of the ships of Alejandro Malaspina, the Spanish explorer who surveyed this area in 1792. Although gold was discovered here and successfully mined by the Spaniards, when their country ceded the region to England, the presence of gold remained a Spanish secret. It was rediscovered a century later, mining began again in the 1920s and the townsite emerged during the mid-1930s. Although inaccessible by road, Zeballos offered most amenities and services of that period, including hotels, well-stocked stores, a bank, a school and a library. By 1939 the population was over 1,500, but the Second World War robbed the mines of skilled labour and by 1943 all had closed. They reopened in 1945 but, with gold pegged at $35 an ounce, they were no longer viable so closed again in 1948. An iron mine that opened in 1962 had closed again by 1969 and the population dropped to 35. Zeballos received a new lease on life when the Tahsis Logging Company established its headquarters there, and construction of the road in 1970 that connected the settlement to the east coast of the Island finally made it accessible by means other than boat or floatplane. Although logging is still the area's major employer, aquaculture and tourism are now important contributors to the economy.

The population of Zeballos now hovers around 260. It has 5 lodges and a hotel, a general store with a liquor outlet, gas pumps, a coin laundry, gift shops and a museum. Of interest to anglers towing their own boats is an excellent all-tide boat ramp with adjacent parking, a government wharf, a fuel dock, and moorage. There is a campsite located about 7 km north of Zeballos, and the BCFS Rhodes Creek campsite is about 7 km south of town on the road to Fair Harbour. This well-shaded site also has a launch ramp and a small dock. If camping, be aware that there is a healthy population of black bears in this area, so take the necessary precautions to prevent encounters.

(Note: The route to Fair Harbour is another 34 km from Zeballos on similar gravel road. It terminates at a parking area for those continuing on by boat to Kyuquot Sound.)

## Weather and Water Conditions

Venz Kuzev operated a commercial troller around northern Vancouver Island for several years before pulling up stakes and moving to Ontario. He eventually relocated in Zeballos in 1996 and the following year built Iris Lodge (named after his wife). (He currently lives in Bulgaria, where

Rock piles and small islands dot the mouth of Esperanza Inlet.

he and Iris have a vineyard.) When we first spoke, Venz described the local weather as "typical west coast of Vancouver Island." This, of course, means that December through February can be wet and windy with occasional short stretches of nice days. Springtime generally starts around late February to early March, but you shouldn't really expect much good weather until mid-April. "Nice" weather begins in May and it can be quite pleasant (with occasional windy disruptions) right through until October when it begins to turn wet and windy again.

Zeballos Inlet is well protected, but the mouth of Esperanza Inlet is exposed to the open Pacific, subjecting it to the whims of offshore wave action that can range from flat calm to downright life-threatening. While prevailing winds are generally north-westerly or southwesterly, during the summer months they tend more to southwesterly or southeasterly. The latter are most prevalent whenever a storm creates a low-pressure system. The wind and water conditions might remain unsettled until early June but usually level out until mid- to late September. Morning fog can be a problem during this warm weather period but it usually burns off before noon.

Doug Ezasiuk (left) of Calgary, Alberta, with 42 pounds of chrome-bright chinook. His guide was Adrian O'Connor.
*Reel Obsession Sport Fishing photo*

## Run Timing

Dan O'Connor and Cristina Lepore own and operate Zeballos Expeditions, which includes Masons Lodge, the Blue Heron Restaurant, Nootka Fishing Charters, kayak rentals, sightseeing cruises, and a land and water taxi service. Cristina, a marine biologist, moved to northern Vancouver Island as a child in 1956. Dan, who became a Zeballos resident in 1992, has established an enviable record as a fishing guide and naturalist. According to him, there is a popular winter-long fishery just out from the Zeballos dock for feeder chinooks that weigh up into the mid-teens.

When the spawning migrations start, sockeye usually appear in Kyuquot Sound about a week prior to moving southward to the area off the mouth of Esperanza Inlet. There they often spend two or three weeks feeding around Catala Island and the cluster of small islands and rocks bordering Gillam Channel and within the mouth of Nuchatlitz Inlet. Eventually the southward-travelling schools will move on while local fish start heading inside toward their home rivers. Depending on the water conditions, they may head upstream immediately to spawn or stage off the estuaries until the first autumn rains raise and cool the rivers.

By the first of July a few large, migratory chinooks start appearing, but these may be spotty for the first week or two until the runs strengthen. This is the period when your chances for trophies of 50 and 60 pounds become very realistic. Mid-July until August 20–25 is the best period for a mixed bag of chinooks and coho.

Strong runs of chum salmon finish off the Zeballos season, appearing around the end of September and thinning out in late November to early December. The same tackle and tactics used for sockeye will take these hard-fighting fish, which average 10 or 11 pounds but occasionally get much larger.

## Hotspots and Tactics

Adrian O'Connor started guiding out of Zeballos in 2000 and formed his own operation, Reel Obsession Sport Fishing, in 2003. He has since established himself as a dependable guide who produces good catches for his customers. He recommends that during the winter and early spring you should try anywhere from Zeballos Inlet out as far as Steamer Point. The standard feeder chinook tactic is downrigging with a white/green hoochie, plug, spoon or medium-sized herring or anchovy, with or without a flasher, at depths of 80 to 150 feet.

Some early season feeder chinooks reach weights approaching 30 pounds.

Around mid-June the sockeye start showing along the surf line off the mouth of Esperanza Inlet, and it is time to try west of Catala Island around Obstruction Reef, Halftide Reef, Outer Black Rock and Low Rock. As they move southward, Middle Reef, Blind Reef, Pin Rock, Nuchatlitz Reef, Danger Rock and Ferrer Point will turn on. When targeting sockeye, try downrigging with small, sparse hoochies in various shades of pink, red or orange rigged 27 inches behind an O'Ki or Hot Spot flasher with orange or red trim. Stick with the standard accepted trolling tactic of going dead slow and in a fairly straight line.

When migratory chinooks start appearing about two weeks later, fish these same areas but move in close around Catala Island and try off Yellow Bluff, Peculiar Point, and through Rolling Roadstead to Black Rock. The southeast side of Gillam Channel can be good, especially around Pin Rock. Ferrer Point, Danger Rock and Nuchatlitz Reef are also popular. As local fish start moving inland toward Zeballos Inlet, concentrate on the area between Centre Island and the mouth of Brodick Creek in Esperanza Inlet and off Steamer Point at the junction with Zeballos Inlet.

There are lots of needlefish and herring present early in the season and matching their size is important. A small herring strip in a teaser works well. From July 1 to September 1, which Adrian O'Connor considers the prime chinook period, trolling anchovies or herring is the most productive tactic. His preference is anchovies in two lengths: 5¼ and 6 inches. His recommended setup consists of a green flasher trailing an anchovy or herring in a Rhys Davis Anchovy Special with two no. 3 treble hooks in tandem. Recommended colours are clear, clear/green, chartreuse, Betsy, chrome, purple haze and blue. When sardines show up, usually around August, larger baits work better. For smaller baits during the early season try leader lengths of 4½ to 6 feet. With larger baits go to 5½ to 7 feet.

Adrian O'Connor often runs one rod without a flasher, usually with a larger bait or lure, and attaches a dummy flasher above the cannonball on a 4-foot-long leader of 100-pound-test line. Light conditions might call for experimenting with the flasher colour. Good patterns are plaid, glow, prism, and

A typical trolling setup includes a flasher and an anchovy in a Rhys Davis Anchovy Special.

silver trimmed with blue, green, red or purple. On cloudy days and later in the season, try a gold flasher.

Lures with dependable track records include hoochies in army truck, octopus, jellyfish, cloverleaf, green ghost and purple haze. If the water is murky, try white or light-coloured glow models. Don't overlook spoons. Good choices are Tomics in no. 158, 395, 403, 512 and 775, Tom Macks in 50/50 nickel/brass, nickel/blue or all nickel, and Coyotes in cop car, glow green, bad attitude, 50/50 silver/green and 50/50 silver/blue. If fishing spoons behind a

Lantzville resident Don Ritter drove across the Island to Zeballos for this trophy chinook.

flasher, experiment with leader lengths of 4½ to 7 feet. Five-inch Tomic plugs can be quite productive at times; best choices include no. 84, 212, 404, 530, 600 and 603.

## AVAILABLE MARINE CHARTS

3604 Nootka Sound to Quatsino Sound
3663 Esperanza Inlet

## Marine Chart Coordinates:

| Place Names: | | Place Names: | |
|---|---|---|---|
| Black Rock | LAT 49°50' LONG 127°02' | Nuchatlitz Reef | LAT 49°46' LONG 126°59' |
| Blind Reef | LAT 49°47' LONG 127°01' | Obstruction Reef | LAT 49°50' LONG 127°05' |
| Brodick Creek | LAT 49°51' LONG 126°54' | Outer Black Rock | LAT 49°49' LONG 127°04' |
| Catala Island | LAT 49°50' LONG 127°03' | Peculiar Point | LAT 49°51' LONG 127°06' |
| Centre Island | LAT 49°51' LONG 126°56' | Pin Rock | LAT 49°47' LONG 127°00' |
| Danger Rock | LAT 49°49' LONG 126°59' | Port Eliza | LAT 49°53' LONG 127°01' |
| Esperanza | LAT 49°52' LONG 126°44' | Queen Cove | LAT 49°53' LONG 126°59' |
| Ferrer Point | LAT 49°45' LONG 126°59' | Rolling Roadstead | LAT 49°51' LONG 127°03' |
| Gillam Channel | LAT 49°48' LONG 127°01' | Rosa Island | LAT 49°" LONG 127°" |
| Halftide Reef | LAT 49°50' LONG 127°05' | Steamer Point | LAT 49°43' LONG 126°48' |
| Kaouk River | LAT 50°04' LONG 127°06' | Tahsis | LAT 49°55' LONG 126°40' |
| Kyuquot Sound | LAT 50°04' LONG 127°13' | Tahsish River | LAT 50°09' LONG 127°06' |
| Little Zeballos | LAT 49°57' LONG 126°49' | Tatchu Point | LAT 49°51' LONG 127°09' |
| Low Rock | LAT 49°48' LONG 127°04' | Yellow Bluff | LAT 49°51' LONG 127°07' |
| Middle Reef | LAT 49°48' LONG 127°02' | Zeballos | LAT 49°59' LONG 126°51' |
| Nootka Island | LAT 49°45' LONG 127°45' | Zeballos Inlet | LAT 49°57' LONG 126°49' |
| Nuchatlitz Inlet | LAT 49°46' LONG 126°56' | Zeballos River | LAT 49°59' LONG 126°51' |

**Our Information Sources**

David Murphy, co-owner, Murphy's
Sport Fishing
Mike Barker, owner, Kyuquot Beach
House
Skip and Susan Plensky, owners, Sea
Otter Lodge
Wayne Moss, former manager,
Walters Cove Lodge
Gail and Richard Leo, owners, Swan
Song Marina

**For visitor information:**

KYUQUOT CHECLESET BAND OFFICE
Kyuquot, BC V0P 1J0
Bus: (250) 332-5259
Fax: (250) 332-5210

Kyuquot Sound is studded with rocks, shallow shoals, islets
and islands, so boaters must always be wary.

## Kyuquot Sound

Kyuquot Sound holds the title of Vancouver Island's most remote community, which is precisely the way most inhabitants like it. Living in
quiet, peaceful surroundings does that to you, especially when your
retreat is situated in what many consider the most beautiful scenery on
the entire West Coast. And if you happen to be an angler—as many of
the local people are—you might think that you have died and gone to
heaven.

Kyuquot Sound is accessible only by air or water. Air Nootka offers
regular scheduled flights from Gold River plus charter flights all year,
and Vancouver Island Air sends almost daily charter flights from
Campbell River during the summer months. Another option that some
find adventurous and interesting is to book passage out of Gold River
on the MV *Uchuck III*, a passenger-carrying coastal freighter that makes
scheduled two-day trips to Kyuquot, departing on Thursdays and
returning on Fridays.

Most visitors get to Kyuquot Sound by driving to Fair Harbour,
which is 34 km beyond Zeballos on a continuation of the gravel road.
The turnoff to Fair Harbour is at the bridge spanning the Zeballos River
just before you enter Zeballos, but we recommend that you drive into
town and gas up your vehicle because there is no vehicle gas available
at Fair Harbour. Although the road from Zeballos to Fair Harbour isn't

any better than that from Highway 19 to Zeballos, it winds through some very scenic country and you will probably encounter black bears, black-tailed deer and possibly some Roosevelt elk along the way.

At Fair Harbour is a Ministry of Tourism, Sports and the Arts campsite, an unpaved boat launch (free), a government dock, a fuel dock selling diesel, marine gas and propane, public parking, and the Swan Song Marina, which also offers some moorage and six private campsites with fresh water and outhouses. Two of their sites are large enough to handle groups. In addition, there is secure parking on the upper level, but it is usually booked up early in the season (as is the moorage).

Marina owners Gail and Richard Leo also operate a general store that offers basic groceries, camping supplies, souvenirs and reasonably priced fishing tackle. Gail Leo warns that they don't always have frozen bait on hand because freezer space is required to supply campers with ice. They are open year round, and while few anglers drive that far for winter chinook fishing, avid halibut anglers appear as early as April. The marina is a great place to drop in for information about which baits and lures are working best, to stock up on them if necessary and determine where the best fishing action has been occurring.

Most of those who tow their own boats to Fair Harbour usually camp there because Kyuquot Sound is only about a half-hour run from the dock. Those without boats should arrange beforehand to be picked up by one of the fishing resorts or water taxis located at Kyuquot Sound.

The area's fishing lodges include Kyuquot Beach House, Murphy's Sport Fishing, Sea Otter Lodge, Slam Bang Lodge and Walters Cove Lodge. There are also bed and breakfast operations and a few cabins available for rent. Anglers interested in camping must do some homework ahead of time. There are 5 marine provincial parks in the area: Big Bunsby (658 ha), Brooks Peninsula (51,631 ha), Dixie Cove (156 ha), Rugged Point (308 ha), and Tahsish-Kwois (10,972 ha). In the village of Kyuquot itself, Mike and Suzy Bostrom operate Kyuquot Market, a small, well-stocked general store that also supplies ice, bait and fishing gear. The only eatery is Miss Charlie's Restaurant, named after Kyuquot's famous pet seal.

The Kyuquot and Checleset bands, northernmost of the 14 Nuu-chah-nulth First Nation bands, control access to many of their traditional territories. Visitors must register at the Kyuquot Checleset Band Office in Houpsitas before venturing onto any of these lands.

The water conditions in Kyuquot Sound range from flat calm to extremely dangerous.

Being located on a main migration path of salmon runs heading south for Esperanza Sound, Nootka Sound and beyond as far as the Columbia River, Kyuquot Sound attracts halibut anglers as early as April, then chinook anglers during June, July, and August, after which the coho action heats up until well into September.

## Weather and Water Conditions

Although spring weather might arrive during early March, wind and water conditions usually remain unsettled until early June and then become more co-operative until mid- to late September. Aside from occasional high winds, the weather is generally pleasant from May until October at which time it turns wet and windy. Heavy rains from November through February are interspaced with stretches of moderate, fairly dry weather.

The open Pacific in this area ranges anywhere from flat calm to extremely dangerous. According to Dave Murphy of Murphy's Sportfishing, nighttime outflow winds can reach gale force or worse without any warning and can be expected at least every other day during the summer. During the summer months the prevailing winds are usually northwesters. Morning fog can be a problem during this warm weather period but it usually burns off before noon.

The Barrier Islands form an arc in front of Kyuquot Sound. Much of this structure is barely submerged, making Kyuquot possibly the most rock-filled sound on the Island's west coast. As running into rocks is an instant way to ruin a fishing trip, it's wise to either hire a guide or travel with someone who has fished there before and knows the area.

The Barrier Islands form an arc in front of Kyuquot Sound.

## Run Timing

Large chinook salmon are called "smileys" for a reason. Lorne Benson took this dandy at Kyuquot Sound while guided by David Murphy.

Although all five species of Pacific salmon return to rivers in Kyuquot Sound, local fish make up a relatively small part of the multitudes that pass by on the "Salmon Highway." Feeder chinooks are present in good numbers all year, and while a few migratory "Columbias" usually appear around late March to early April, the main fishing season for chinooks and halibut is traditionally from June through August, followed by a very active September fishery for coho and then chums later on.

Some early sockeye might start showing in early June, but July is usually their peak. As these runs stay farther offshore, they don't receive much attention from recreational anglers. The chinook, coho and pink runs continue building, and by July there should be plenty of trophy-sized chinooks in the mix. The season's largest fish are usually caught in August, with a few stragglers still showing in early September. Large northern coho move into the area in September along with the first chums, and the latter provide tackle-punishing action pretty well through October.

## Hotspots and Tactics

Anyone who has fished Kyuquot Sound will usually state that when the bite is on, virtually anything you put in the water catches fish. It's simply a matter of determining the depth where your target species is feeding and then presenting your offering. The most

Washington resident Tom Graham connected with this trophy chinook at Kyuquot Sound while guided by David Murphy. *Murphy Sportfishing photo*

common tactic is downrigging with bait, hoochies, spoons or plugs, but a lot of light tackle enthusiasts do well with drift-jigs, and since the early 1980s some hard-core fly fishers have been listing Kyuquot as a "must go to" destination. Jim Crawford, author of *Salmon to a Fly*, started going there in 1983 and claims it's possibly the best place on the Island's west coast to hook big chinooks and halibut on cast flies. That you can also catch trophy-sized coho goes without saying.

If you decide to try for sockeye, downrig with small, sparse hoochies in various shades of pink, red or orange placed 27 inches behind a silver or pearlescent white flasher with orange or red trim. For chinooks and coho, your collection of hoochies should include black/white, green/white, glow green, purple haze, cotton candy, jellyfish, watermelon and Halloween. A few of the favourite flashers include Hot Spots in green/silver, golden warrior and plaid Mylar, and O'Ki Big Shooters in army truck and purple haze.

For anchovies, use a Rhys Davis Anchovy Special in watermelon, bloody nose, glow, glow green, and chrome purple/gold. For herring, a Super Herring Special in clear, clear green, chrome blue/green, and chrome green/chartreuse. Spoons, fished with or without a flasher, are popular throughout the season, especially Coyotes in cop car, glow green, silver/green, and silver/blue, and 3½- to 6-inch Tomics in no.

Big plugs attract big chinooks.
*Murphy Sportfishing photo*

158, 403 and 512. For plugs, consider the "big lure/big fish" adage and try Tomic Classics in lengths from 5 to 7 inches. Good choices are no. 212, 404, 600 and 603.

Lookout Island is one of the most popular areas mainly because schools of chinooks pass through continuously all summer. Other popular spots are the islands off Rugged Point and around the Thornton Islands where schools of herring are usually found. At "The Wall" near Racoon Point, the shallow bottom drops sharply to about 120 feet, which means good prospects for chinooks and halibut. Kyuquot Reef offers protected fishing among its kelp beds and small islands and is a good place to head if the wind picks up.

While much of the fishing is fairly close to shore and around various kelp beds, when the open Pacific is co-operative, those with fast, seaworthy boats can run out to a reef about 15 km from the Mission Group. Located in about 200 feet of water, it rises up fairly sharply to within 100 feet of the surface. It's worth noting that, being so close to the continental shelf, it's a whole new world out there. In addition to the usual assortment of sea birds and ducks, depending on the location you might also see puffins, pigeon guillemots, rhinoceros auklets, and even an occasional albatross gliding in from far beyond the continental

Sea otters are currently quite common in the Kyuquot Sound area.

shelf. Sea otters are now fairly common throughout the area, as are sea lions and grey whales.

## AVAILABLE MARINE CHARTS

3604 Nootka Sound to Quatsino Sound
3623 Kyuquot Sound to Cape Cook
3682 Kyuquot Sound

## Marine Chart Coordinates:

| Place Names: | | Place Names: | |
| --- | --- | --- | --- |
| Barrier Islands | LAT 49°57' LONG 127°19' | Kyuquot Sound | LAT 50°04' LONG 127°13' |
| Big Bunsby MPP | LAT 50°06' LONG 127°30' | Mission Group | LAT 50°00' LONG 127°24' |
| Brooks Peninsula MPP | LAT 50°10' LONG 127°45' | Racoon Point | LAT 49°59' LONG 127°18' |
| Checleset Bay | LAT 50°06' LONG 127°40' | Rugged Point MPP | LAT 49°58' LONG 127°15' |
| Clanninick Creek | LAT 50°03' LONG 127°24' | Solander Island | LAT 50°07' LONG 127°56' |
| Copp Island | LAT 50°03' LONG 127°11' | Spring Island | LAT 50°00' LONG 127°25' |
| Dixie Cove MPP | LAT 50°03' LONG 127°12' | Tahsish River | LAT 50°09' LONG 127°06' |
| Double Island | LAT 49°51' LONG 127°00' | Tahsish-Kwois MPP | LAT 50°06' LONG 127°07' |
| Fair Harbour | LAT 50°04' LONG 127°07' | Thornton Islands | LAT 49°58' LONG 127°20' |
| Hohoae Island | LAT 50°03' LONG 127°13' | Thornton Reef | LAT 50°56' LONG 127°46' |
| Houpsitas | LAT 50°02' LONG 127°22' | Union Island | LAT 50°01' LONG 127°16' |
| Kyuquot | LAT 50°02' LONG 127°22' | Walters Cove | LAT 50°02' LONG 127°22' |
| Kyuquot Bay | LAT 49°59' LONG 127°18' | West Rocks | LAT 49°58' LONG 127°18' |
| Kyuquot Channel | LAT 49°59' LONG 127°15' | | |

# Clayoquot Sound

The west coast of Vancouver Island is a confusion of island-cluttered sounds that branch into long, narrow, tortuous inlets. Of the five major sounds, many people consider Clayoquot the most beautiful and awe-inspiring, especially in those areas exposed to the open Pacific where high swells break into white-capped surf that beats relentlessly against

The view from Tofino Harbour toward Catface Mountain overlooking Clayoquot Sound.

**Our Information Sources**

Dick Close, former owner Weigh West
Marine Resort
Jason Mohl, Jay's Clayoquot Ventures

**For visitor information:**

TOFINO VISITOR CENTRE
Box 249
1426 Pacific Rim Highway
Tofino, BC  V0R 2Z0
(250) 725-3414
info@tourismtofino.com
www.tourismtofino.com

the rugged jumble of islands, rock piles and reefs. It is the type of water usually avoided by prudent boaters, but this is not the case in Clayoquot Sound. Blame it on the fish—chinook, coho and halibut to be precise—that you will find there in abundance if your timing is right.

Clayoquot Sound is also the most popular tourist destination on Vancouver Island's west coast, attracting over a million visitors annually. Legions go to simply walk the smooth, sandy beaches, dig a feed of tasty razor clams, observe the profusion of wading and sea birds, hike the bordering forest trails, or challenge the booming breakers with surfboards or kayaks. Other popular activities include offshore boat tours to observe humpback whales and Pacific grey whales on their annual migration north from Baja California to the Bering and Chukchi seas; sailing, cruising or ocean kayaking the waters surrounding Meares, Vargas and Flores islands; or travelling 65 km northwest by boat or floatplane to bathe in the steaming pools of Hot Springs Cove near the mouth of Sidney Inlet.

Headquarters for all these pastimes is Tofino, a community of about 2,000 permanent residents. Located on the tip of Esowista Peninsula, it is the most westerly point on Highway 4, which winds westward from the Inland Island Highway at Parksville via Port Alberni. A number of resorts, vacation rentals, hotels and motels offer a full range of accommodations; there are also several bed and breakfast operations, and virtually hundreds of campsites. Nevertheless, starting in early March, visitors should make advance reservations for weekends and spring school breaks. By July, reservations are an absolute must, and during August and early September every available type of accommodation is filled to capacity.

There are two public boat-launching ramps in the area. The main ramp is right in Tofino at the 4th Street Harbour, while the rustic Grice Bay ramp is in nearby Pacific Rim National Park. Moorage can be limited from June through August, with the Fisherman's Dock on 4th Street, the Crab Dock on Olsen Road, and Weigh West Marina providing the best options. Method Marine off Main Street has the town's only gas dock, and its marina is used primarily by local residents. Finding parking space for your boat trailer can be challenging, so check for a designated space before you launch.

Long-time resident Dick Close, the former owner of Weigh West Marine Resort, advises visitors that while the marine area is well marked with navigation aids, you must watch for hazards like the sandbars off Beck Island, which are exposed at low tide, or Elbow Bank on the west side of Maurus Channel, which has only a foot or so of water over it at low tide. Another hazard is provided by local crab traps: if the water is choppy, their floats and ropes floating on the surface will be barely visible and they can damage propellers.

For inshore boating a 16- to 18-footer is suitable for most popular hotspots. It should contain the compulsory safety equipment, an area marine chart, a compass, a VHF radio and a depth sounder. For offshore fishing add a Global Positioning System to cope with fog.

The ideal offshore boat is at least 20 feet long with a deep-V hull and a high bow. If using an open boat, expect to get wet because even moderate winds create a cross-chop on incoming swells, making it impossible to avoid taking in water. Survival suits and rubber boots are an absolute must in order to keep dry and warm, especially in an open boat. Visitors with their own boats are wise to hire a guide for at least one day. This is money well spent as they will learn how to get around the area, where to fish, and which techniques are productive.

## Weather and Water Conditions

Despite an annual rainfall hovering around 125 inches a year, Tofino enjoys the warmest average temperature in Canada. Historical patterns show that most heavy rains fall during November, December and February. There are stretches of moderate weather in January, March

Looking across Chesterman's Beach to Lennard Island Lighthouse, a welcome entrance to Clayoquot Sound. *Jay's Clayoquot Ventures photo*

and April, but from then on it is anyone's guess whether there will be rain or sun, and weather swings are usually on extremely short notice.

The prevailing westerlies blow at about 20 km/h, which is not a problem for seaworthy boats, but during summer highs most storms are southeasters, and they can be nasty. Fortunately, Clayoquot Sound has protected areas that can be fished during heavy westerly or southeasterly blows.

July and August are bad for fog, which is easily handled in boats outfitted with suitable electronics. Although not recommended, some boaters lacking sophisticated navigational equipment do venture offshore in foggy conditions by buddying up with boats that are properly equipped; however, it is imperative that they stay in visual contact with each other throughout the trip and maintain radio contact.

If you are prone to seasickness, be warned that offshore fishing here involves virtually non-stop up-and-down mixed with persistent side-to-side movement. Swells from the open Pacific are consistent and there is usually a cross-chop. This makes for very uncomfortable fishing, and at times even seasoned sailors turn varying shades of green. Knowing that anglers will endure almost anything in order to catch fish, most stores in Tofino carry good stocks of anti-seasick wristbands, ear patches and non-prescription medications.

## Run Timing

Jason Mohl, owner of Jay's Clayoquot Ventures, worked as a commercial fisherman and seafood processor before switching to the recreational sector in Clayoquot Sound. That was in 1995, and since then he has accrued a wealth of knowledge and experience about this area and its fish and wildlife. According to Mohl, while there are good numbers of juvenile feeder chinooks available throughout the winter months, especially in the northwestern section of Clayoquot Sound, they receive relatively little fishing effort because of adverse weather conditions. Things start to perk up about mid-April when migratory chinooks move southward down the coast, feeding actively along the way. Generally, however, most of the action remains offshore

Jason Mohl guides guests to chinooks like this trophy fish every season. *Jay's Clayoquot Ventures photo*

throughout May, by which time chinooks are in the 14- to 35-pound range and halibut about 20 to 60 pounds. In early June some chinooks should start moving inside as will a few southward-migrating coho weighing up to 8 or 9 pounds. An added bonus occasionally occurs when schools of needlefish move inside to spawn and the chinooks follow them. This provides exciting action for salmon of 10 to 25 pounds, but such events are undependable and entirely at the whim of the needlefish.

By July many chinooks are inshore around the islands where protected and generally shallow waters—15 to 30 feet deep on average—provide a safe, productive area for them as well as for early season coho. August is considered the prime month for the Robertson Creek chinook run. This large concentration of fish ranges up to 45 pounds and occasionally larger and normally remains in the area for a month or more before moving on into Alberni Inlet.

Migratory chinooks are pretty well finished after the Labour Day weekend, but coho fishing can stay good until mid-October. With their size and numbers increasing daily, fly fishers and light tackle anglers are in seventh heaven. Although there are runs of sockeye and chums inside Clayoquot Sound, virtually no one fishes for them, probably because there are still so many chinooks and coho available. Pink salmon, which migrate past well offshore, are also ignored.

Jay's Clayoquot Ventures guide Blake Klopfenstein with the sort of chinook salmon that he often produces for his guests while fishing out of Tofino.

## Hotspots and Tactics

During the winter months, mostly due to uncooperative weather, feeder chinooks receive relatively little fishing pressure. However, most inshore waters are protected by islands and reefs, making them suitable for small boats and, weather permitting, you can try around Shelter Inlet, Sidney Inlet and Hot Springs Cove. Offshore, Rafael Point and Portland Point are also productive.

With the arrival of the first migratory chinooks, fishing action starts about 5 to 8 km offshore, primarily on the banks off Rafael Point and Portland Point, which by this time have been yielding bottom fish for a month or so. The bank off Rafael Point is about 5 km west of the Russell Channel mouth and appears on the marine chart as a small, irregularly shaped shoal showing 37 metres at the western end and 40 metres at the eastern end.

Early season offshore tactics consist primarily of downrigging or trolling close to the bottom with anchovies, cut-plug herring or large hoochies. Drift-jigging is also popular and productive, with the lure's colour dependent on the light conditions, and its size and weight on the boat's speed of drift. A selection ranging from 2 to 8 ounces will handle most situations with good colour selections being silver, white or pearl in combinations with green, blue, mauve, pink, red or grey. An anchovy or medium-sized herring trailed 6 to 7 feet behind a flasher is often the gear of choice as this gives anglers a shot at halibut as well as chinooks, but some rely on 7-inch Tomic plugs or spoons in glow patterns like the O'Ki Titan or the Gibbs Gator.

When chinooks are near shore, the most popular spot is Wilf Rock, a pile of rocks located just outside the surf line and only 10 minutes from downtown Tofino. Other hotspots are the rock pile farther west called the La Croix Group, Bartlett Island and Blunden Island. Some areas where baitfish schools tend to congregate are quite shallow—12 to 16 feet—making them excellent for drift-jigging and casting flies. Bait also congregates around Ahous Point, Cleland Island and Plover Reefs, but these spots seldom get much effort despite the presence of fish.

Two islands in Brabant Channel—Hobbs and Burgess—offer excellent fishing, and Coomes Bank in Calmus Passage is good on flood tides. Bartlett Island is surrounded by small islets and rocks and the seaward side has some small bays worth checking out. Much of the water depth is about 30 feet around Russell Channel, Kutcous Point and the Kutcous Islets at the southern tip of Flores Island. And if you have time and feel like exploring, there is good fishing along the Hot Springs Cove side of Flores Island. It takes about 90 minutes to get there in a fast boat but the fishing is considered well worth the trip.

Whenever baitfish appear inshore, drift-jigging can be very productive for coho and chinooks. If there are no big tide changes, try lures in the 2- to 3-ounce range. Those trimmed with green or grey work well if herring or anchovies are present, and mauve works if there are needlefish.

In August inshore chinook fishing is evenly divided between trolling and motor-mooching. Cut-plug herring is a popular bait but most of the time anchovies will outfish everything. Some anglers do well by simply trolling a cut-plug herring or anchovy behind their downrigger without a holder or flasher. If added attraction is desired, try a clear or chartreuse Rhys Davis Anchovy Special with an anchovy and trail it behind either a Hot Spot flasher or Les Davis dodger. They work equally well, but while colour doesn't seem to matter, leader length does. Try 4 to 6 feet on a flasher and down to 12 inches on a no. 0 dodger. Try them in reliable areas like Wilf Rock, "the Glory Hole," and Tree, Blunden and Bartlett islands.

Fly fishers love this time of the year for it seems like anything thrown at feeding coho results in violent strikes. Good patterns include Epoxy Needlefish and chartreuse Clayoquot Clousers. In addition to salmon, you can try for sporty black rockfish, greenling, lingcod and cabezon around most kelp beds and line-sizzling Pacific mackerel whenever the El Niño current swings in close to the western coastline. The latter is a case of making the best of a bad situation as mackerel are a real nuisance to salmon anglers.

An olive/white Clayoquot Clouser is one of the most popular fly patterns for this area.

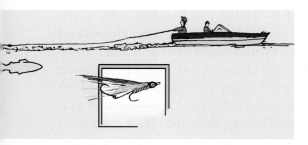

While bucktailing, the rod can be hand held or placed in a holder. Either way, it should ride right on or just beneath the surface.

Typical bucktails used for high-speed trolling are tied using two prime colours like this purple/white pattern.

Bucktailing and skip-fly fishing can be very productive from June until mid-October, but coho can be frustratingly selective about the colour, size and speed of a fly. Try patterns that incorporate white with pink, orange, green, mauve or grey, preferably with a few strands of Krystal Flash or Flashabou on the sides. Start with 5- to 7-inch-long bucktails trolled about 15 to 25 feet behind the boat, either right on or slightly below the surface. If coho charge a fly but refuse to hit, the colour and trolling speed are probably good, so try a shorter pattern. Some anglers simply use scissors to trim an inch or so off the one already on their line.

Gear anglers targeting inshore coho can troll with small spoons like the Gibbs Gypsy or Lucky Dog or with a needlefish or plankton hoochie behind an O'Ki Lil Shooter or Gibbs flasher. Drift-jiggers can expect success with a Gibbs Minnow or Zzinger. Another exhilarating light tackle method is mooching with a live needlefish and the lightest sinker possible. This often produces great action at Catface Bar, Tonquin Island and "Bullshit Pass" (Bartlett Island).

Later, after coho have moved well into Clayoquot Sound, try Tofino Inlet, the Kennedy River mouth (watch for the closure boundaries in Kennedy Cove), Matlset Narrows on the back of Meares Island and Dawley Passage at the bottom end of Fortune Channel. These are also good spots to head whenever westerlies start blowing, but bear in mind that a non-retention of chinooks goes into effect on August 1. Good areas on a flood tide are Kutcous Point, Chetarpe and "Bullshit Pass."

The reliably good weather in September creates some of the entire season's most pleasant fishing conditions. By the second or third week the number of large migratory chinooks starts thinning, but offshore waters often continue providing a mix of mature and juvenile chinooks right through late October. Switch to trolling smaller flashers with Gibbs Gypsy, Lucky Dog or needlefish spoons, squirts or hoochies and Wee-Tad Tomic plugs. After the Labour Day weekend coho fishing usually stays good around Coomes Bank, Monks Islet, Clifford Point, Russell Channel, Hobbs and Burgess islands, inside and off both sides of Bartlett Island, Wilf Rock, Wickaninnish Island, the bottom end of Duffin Passage and Lennard Island.

After fishing out of Tofino, Doug and Duncan Armitage returned home to Calgary, AB, with this trophy chinook. *Jay's Clayoquot Ventures photo*

## AVAILABLE MARINE CHART

3640 Clayoquot Sound

## Marine Chart Coordinates:

| Place Names: | | Place Names: | |
| --- | --- | --- | --- |
| Ahous Point | LAT 49°10' LONG 126°01' | Hot Springs Cove | LAT 49°22' LONG 126°16' |
| Bartlett Island | LAT 49°13' LONG 126°05' | Kennedy River | LAT 49°08' LONG 125°40' |
| Blunden Island | LAT 49°11' LONG 126°03' | Kutcous Islets | LAT 49°15' LONG 126°04' |
| Burgess Islet | LAT 49°13' LONG 126°02' | Kutcous Point | LAT 49°15' LONG 126°05' |
| "Bullshit Pass" | LAT 49°13' LONG 126°04' | La Croix Group | LAT 49°09' LONG 126°00' |
| "Catface Shoal" | LAT 49°13' LONG 125°58' | Lennard Island | LAT 49°07' LONG 125°55' |
| Chetarpe | LAT 48°15' LONG 126°00' | Matlset Narrows | LAT 49°14' LONG 125°48' |
| "Chicken Ranch" | LAT 48°57' LONG 126°01' | Monks Islet | LAT 49°14' LONG 126°01' |
| Cleland Island | LAT 49°10' LONG 126°05' | Offshore Bank (Rafael Point) | LAT 49°14' LONG 126°14' |
| Clifford Point | LAT 49°17' LONG 126°02' | Plover Reefs | LAT 49°11' LONG 126°05' |
| Coomes Bank | LAT 49°13' LONG 126°00' | Portland Point | LAT 49°04' LONG 125°49' |
| Dawley Passage | LAT 49°09' LONG 125°48' | Rafael Point | LAT 49°17' LONG 126°14' |
| Duffin Passage | LAT 49°09' LONG 125°55' | Russell Channel | LAT 49°14' LONG 126°06' |
| Esowista Peninsula | LAT 49°05' LONG 125°50' | "Three Humps" | LAT 49°00' LONG 125°56' |
| "Glory Hole" | LAT 48°08' LONG 125°59' | Tofino Inlet | LAT 49°09' LONG 125°40' |
| Heisen Bank | LAT 48°54' LONG 125°54' | Wickaninnish Island | LAT 49°08' LONG 125°56' |
| Hobbs Islet | LAT 49°12' LONG 126°02' | Wilf Rock | LAT 49°08' LONG 125°29' |

# Ucluelet

Whether you pronounce it Yoo-cloo-let or—as most residents prefer—Yoo-clet, many saltwater anglers from around the world agree that Ucluelet is a great place for a fishing holiday. Barkley Sound's abundance of herring, anchovy, needlefish, squid and crustaceans make it a

A breakwater in Ucluelet Harbour.

**Our Information Sources**

Norm Reite, former owner, Island West Resort
Bill von Brendel, owner, Just Fish'n Guide Service

**For visitor information:**

UCLUELET VISITOR CENTRE
Box 428
2791 Pacific Rim Highway
Ucluelet, BC V0R 3A0
(250) 726-4600
pacificrimvisitorcentre@telus.net
www.pacificrimvisitor.ca

major year-round feeding ground. In addition, it borders on a major migration route of southern chinook salmon stocks, including those from the Columbia and Fraser rivers, and from mid-July through August it receives a tremendous influx of salmon returning to Robertson Creek Hatchery, backbone of the world-famous Alberni Inlet chinook fishery. Add to all of this a bounty of bottom fish, and one can appreciate why Barkley Sound is a "must visit" destination for so many anglers.

Road access to Ucluelet, which is located on the Ucluth Peninsula at the northwestern corner of Barkley Sound, is via Pacific Rim Highway No. 4, about a two-hour scenic drive from the new Inland Highway junction at Qualicum Beach. The peninsula overlooks sweeping, ruggedly beautiful seascapes, and the area's abundance and diversity of marine wildlife attracts nature lovers from around the world.

Ucluelet is also accessible by boat from Bamfield, near the southeast corner of Barkley Sound, and from Port Alberni via a 40-km run down Alberni Inlet. From there it is about an equal distance to the outer islands of the Broken Group, central of three components of Pacific Rim National Park.

## Weather and Water Conditions

The main caveat to all the good fishing in this area is weather, which is typical West Coast—if you don't like it, wait five minutes for it to change. Winter rains and high winds often shut down offshore fishing for several days at a stretch, and spring conditions can be similar, albeit warmer. The summer months are generally good, but as this area faces the open Pacific, keeping a sharp weather watch is strongly recommended. And be warned that fog becomes fairly consistent starting in August.

The offshore banks are not for inexperienced or improperly equipped boaters. West Coast weather can be changeable, uncomfortable and—that far offshore—unforgiving. In addition to standard safety equipment and foul weather clothing, a well-equipped boat should carry marine charts of the area, a compass and a VHF radio. Smaller boats seldom have radar but a Global Positioning System will lead you home should the fog roll in—and it also makes relocating the banks easier.

Wash rocks, common along the outer perimeter of Barkley Sound, are often good places to try for salmon.

If using your own boat—assuming it is large enough, seaworthy, and properly equipped—the simplest procedure is to follow the recreational fishing fleet out in the morning and then stay with them. But never assume that, if it suddenly turns foggy, you can follow the fleet back for there is no guarantee they will be visible. This is where a GPS can be a lifesaver.

Norm Reite, former owner of Island West Resort, offers this solid advice to visitors planning to use their own boats: "This is a tremendous place to visit and you can have a great time with your own boat—but it's not for the inexperienced. These are exposed waters, and there are reefs and rock piles where good fishing is going to draw you in close to them. In order to avoid tragedies, you have to use common sense. That's a major component when you are fishing anywhere, but even more so out here. Another point is that if you have your boat serviced just before coming here, dump it into your home waters and do your sea trial there. I wish I had a nickel for everyone who has had their boat serviced, then brought it over here and discovered something is screwed up. It happens a lot."

## Run Timing

Bill von Brendel's knowledge and experience have earned him an enviable reputation among fellow guides and a satisfying number of

Fishing guide Bill von Brendel tempted this chinook with an anchovy in a Rhys Davis Anchovy Special.

repeat customers. He advises that, weather and sea conditions permitting, Barkley Sound provides good winter fishing for resident feeder chinooks. January and February are good for feeders inside Barkley Sound, and then larger chinooks appear on the offshore banks in March and April. In May much of the chinook action moves offshore, and by month's end sockeye should start showing up inside the Sound. The offshore action continues throughout June, but some chinooks head inshore prior to running up Alberni Inlet around month's end. Sockeye start moving into the inlet about mid-June. This early season action improves steadily with the arrival of migratory salmon throughout June, July and August, followed by an excellent fall fishery for coho and usually the largest chinooks of the year.

Offshore chinook action continues in July, and there is a mixed bag fishery in Barkley Sound for chinooks, coho and sockeye, with sockeye thinning out in August. By mid- to late September migratory chinooks have moved upstream but coho action remains good until mid-October. Feeders then provide the remainder of the winter salmon fishery.

The spring herring spawn produces wild-paced fishing. As the mature herring are fairly large, the salmon feeding on them are some of the largest found in any early season fishery on the Island's west coast, often averaging between the high teens and low twenties.

Some time between late May and July squid move inshore to spawn, though pinpointing the time is impossible as it varies so greatly. In recent years their numbers have declined, possibly as a result of El Niño

## Rigging a Live Squid

Bill von Brendel uses a sliding tandem setup with a no. 2 single hook in front and a no. 4 treble behind, about 6 to 8 feet of 20-pound-test leader, and a sinker of 1 to 2 ounces. You will need to adjust the sliding single so the treble is about centred on the tentacles and then carefully hook the squid through the top of its cape. The treble is allowed to hang freely. Let out enough line so the squid is about 3 feet

from the bottom then place your rod in a holder. When your rod tip starts dancing erratically from the squid's swimming action, get ready. . .

Von Brendel said that he keeps a few of these rigs tied up and stored in plastic bags in his tackle box for ready use whenever schools of squid are spotted. "They might sit there for five years," he added, "but when you see squid you want to be ready for them."

effects, but when they do appear, so do some big chinooks. Unfortunately, this can be an undependable fishery because, while squid might produce fast-paced fishing one day, the chinooks might totally ignore them the following day. Light-coloured plugs, hoochies and drift-jigs are good lure choices, but some anglers prefer mooching or trolling with live squid that they catch with a squid jig or a white Buzz Bomb.

Tom Stefanyk with his "chromer" chinook caught while fishing out of Ucluelet.

## Offshore Hotspots and Tactics

Banks located 6 to 30 km offshore from Ucluelet include South Bank (6 to 10 km offshore), Lighthouse Bank (8 to 10 km), The Wreck (16 km) and Big Bank (32 km). Some of these are not very well defined and in a few cases appear to be little more than a meeting of opposing currents. When large numbers of feeder chinooks are attracted to the banks by massive concentrations of baitfish, anglers may enjoy non-stop action for hours on end. Baitfish usually congregate along the edges and down the sides of drop-offs where salmon are often found at 115 to 180 feet and occasionally as deep as 250 feet. Depending on baitfish and squid movements, the action usually starts heading inshore in June.

Downrigging is the preferred winter chinook tactic. Popular setups include a herring or anchovy in a green or clear Rhys Davis Anchovy Special with or without a flasher or dodger. Popular flashers are Hot Spot, O'Ki, Abe & Al, and no. 2 or 3 Pal dodgers. Other lures worth trying include various hoochies, Hot Spot Apex, and large Tom Mack and Coyote spoons. Also productive are 5- to 7-inch-long Tomic plugs in models 55, 158 and 232.

## Inshore Hotspots

Although the banks continue producing salmon, near the end of July the chinooks start moving inshore, making them closer to access throughout August and well into

Trolling for chinooks and coho with large spoons has increased in popularity in recent years.

September. Some of the season's best fishing starts as increasing numbers of migratory chinooks appear between Long Beach and Ucluelet, mainly around Florencia Bay. The best spots are just outside the kelp line, close to where swells crash endlessly against the rocks.

Wya Point, Little Beach and Florencia Island can be good as early as June but start getting stronger in July. From about mid-July to the second or third week of September fishing is traditionally done along the shoreline with herring or anchovies with or without a flasher. If mackerel are present due to El Niño, switch to Tomic plugs that match the bait in size and colour. Fishing this close to shore can be extremely dangerous because of the high swells from the open Pacific, so you should remain well outside the foam-ringed reefs bordering the shoreline. Stay attentive to other boats in the area as you will probably be manoeuvring in extremely close quarters. This is neither the time nor place to be rigging a rod or tying hook setups, so prepare all of your equipment prior to heading out.

## Barkley Sound Hotspots

The protected waters inside Barkley Sound don't require the same level of skills and high-tech navigational equipment necessary for offshore fishing. Most early chinooks caught here are mint bright but by late August usually start darkening.

Early season fishing is generally around inshore rock piles like Mara, Great Bear, Alley and Sail and around the George Fraser Islands. Herring initially start appearing in January and spawning begins at

This picturesque stretch of shoreline typifies why anglers should always carry a camera when they go fishing.

some point in March or April. Fishing continues around the rock piles until late April, and when the herring move offshore again, the anglers follow them out.

During the spring, herring frequently appear just off the Ucluelet Harbour mouth, attracting chinooks to within easy reach of town. While there is never any guarantee they will spawn so close to Ucluelet (or when), major areas within reasonable running distance are Mayne Bay and Toquart Bay, about 17 km northeast. Other spawning areas are Vernon Bay at the top end of Imperial Eagle Channel and Rainy Bay near the mouth of Alberni Inlet; however, the herring may decide to use any stretch of shallow water located along the shoreline.

Just outside of Ucluelet Inlet in Newcombe Channel, try the bay between Beg Island and the Food Islets, the west side of Starlight Reef to Mara Rock (locally called "Black Rock") and the west side of Great Bear Rock across to Alley Rock. In May and June, then again in late August and early September, try the shoreline between the Food Islets and Forbes Island.

The Broken Group, consisting of over 100 islands and islets, provides its best fishing from June through August. A good stretch for trolling is northeast to southwest along the outside edge of the rocky structure between the Pigot Islets and Lovett Island and hard in against the outside edge of Drum Rocks. Cree Island is quite reliable with most trophy-sized chinooks taken there in early August. Troll its eastern side in a circular loop that is framed by reefs to the north and east. Off Effingham Island, try around Meares Bluff and along the south side as far as Cree Island. Effingham's north side is also good and it is sheltered from offshore winds. Closer to the mouth of Alberni Inlet around Swale Rock and south to Turner Islet the fishing is good from late July through August.

Much of the June and July action is often right on the surface, and then starting in June one or more runs of large chinooks arrive with several more runs following. One June run has fish weighing 30 to 40 pounds, offering the prospect of spending an entire day (or more) catching

Co-author Larry Stefanyk with a chinook taken while guided out of Ucluelet by Bill von Brendel.

nothing but tyee-class fish—often as fast as your baits hit the water.

Rainy Bay is prime for big chinooks from August until as late as mid-September, depending on when the first autumn rains attract them into Alberni Inlet. Try the deep west arm around to the south side of the Boyson Islands and along either side of Chup Point. About mid-September some anglers move back offshore again where they encounter large, late-running coho and some nice-sized feeder chinooks.

## AVAILABLE MARINE CHARTS

3602 Approaches to Juan de Fuca Strait
3603 Ucluelet Inlet to Nootka Sound
3646 Plans—Barkley Sound (Bamfield Inlet, Ucluelet Inlet, Uchucklesit Inlet, Fatty Basin)
3668 Alberni Inlet (Port Alberni, Robbers Passage)
3670 Broken Group
3671 Barkley Sound

## Marine Chart Coordinates:

| Place Names: | | Place Names: | |
|---|---|---|---|
| Alberni Inlet | LAT 49°05' LONG 124°50' | Lovett Island | LAT 48°54' LONG 125°22' |
| Alley Rock | LAT 48°54' LONG 125°26' | Mara Rock | LAT 48°53' LONG 125°29' |
| Barkley Sound | LAT 48°51' LONG 125°23' | Mayne Bay | LAT 48°59' LONG 125°19' |
| Beg Islands | LAT 48°55' LONG 125°30' | Meares Bluff | LAT 48°52' LONG 125°17' |
| Big (La Pérouse) Bank | LAT 48°45' LONG 125°55' | Pigot Islets | LAT 48°53' LONG 125°24' |
| "Black Rock" | LAT 48°53' LONG 125°29' | Newcombe Channel | LAT 48°55' LONG 125°29' |
| Boyson Islands | LAT 48°58' LONG 125°02' | Rainy Bay | LAT 48°58' LONG 125°02' |
| Broken Group | LAT 48°54' LONG 125°20' | "Red Can" | LAT 48°54' LONG 125°32' |
| Chup Point | LAT 48°57' LONG 125°02' | Sail Rock | LAT 48°53' LONG 125°24' |
| Cree Island | LAT 48°51' LONG 125°20' | Starlight Reef | LAT 48°53' LONG 125°29' |
| Drum Rocks | LAT 48°54' LONG 125°23' | Southwest Corner | LAT 48°50' LONG 125°49' |
| Effingham Island | LAT 48°52' LONG 125°19' | Swale Rock | LAT 48°55' LONG 125°13' |
| Florencia Bay | LAT 48°59' LONG 125°38' | Toquart Bay | LAT 49°01' LONG 125°00' |
| Food Islets | LAT 48°55' LONG 125°29' | Turner Islet | LAT 48°55' LONG 125°14' |
| Forbes Island | LAT 48°57' LONG 125°25' | Ucluelet | LAT 48°56' LONG 125°33' |
| George Fraser Islands | LAT 48°54' LONG 125°31' | Ucluelet Inlet | LAT 48°57' LONG 125°32' |
| Great Bear Rock | LAT 48°53' LONG 125°27' | Ucluth Peninsula | LAT 48°57' LONG 125°35' |
| Imperial Eagle Channel | LAT 48°54' LONG 125°12' | Vernon Bay | LAT 48°59' LONG 125°09' |
| La Pérouse Bank | LAT 48°45' LONG 125°55' | "The Wreck" | LAT 48°44' LONG 125°53' |
| Lighthouse Bank | LAT 48°52' LONG 125°38' | Wya Point | LAT 48°58' LONG 125°37' |
| Long Beach | LAT 49°03' LONG 125°43' | | |

# Alberni Inlet

Port Alberni is located at the top end of Alberni Inlet, a 48-kilometre-long channel that averages barely 1 to 2 km wide. This is also where the Somass River enters the Inlet, and it is upstream on the Somass's main tributary, the Stamp River, that the Robertson Creek Hatchery was established in 1960 at the outlet of Great Central Lake. Since its opening, this federal hatchery has been the most successful operation on Vancouver Island and is considered the most resounding success story in the history of North American salmonid enhancement. Annual smolt production averages 7 million chinooks, 500,000 coho and 130,000 steelhead. Returns average 80,000 chinooks, 40,000 coho and 5,000 steelhead.

### Our Information Sources

Al Ehrenberg, owner, Gone Fishin', Port Alberni
David Murphy, co-owner, Murphy Sportfishing, Port Alberni
Marilyn Murphy, co-owner, Murphy Sportfishing, Port Alberni
Jake Leyenaar, owner, Jake's Charters, Port Alberni

### For visitor information:

ALBERNI VALLEY VISITOR CENTRE
2533 Redford Street
Port Alberni, BC V9Y 8P2
(250) 724-6535
(866) 576-3662
avcoc@alberni.net
www.avcoc.com

In addition to the hatchery, fertilization projects on Sproat and Great Central lakes pump over 16 million sockeye into the Somass system each year. As sockeye returns might vary from less than a half million to over a million fish annually, DFO adjusts retention limits accordingly. During a typical year anglers usually plan on keeping four sockeye daily but this might plunge to zero during a poor return year.

With such an abundance of salmon and steelhead returning to Alberni Inlet, recreational fishing rates high as an economic driver in the Alberni Valley, and Port Alberni has become a world-famous sport fishing destination. A modern, cosmopolitan city, it offers a full range of accommodations and services. There are 11 hotels and motels (3 with campgrounds), 5 other campgrounds, 3 resorts and a dozen or so bed and breakfast operations. Finding accommodations is seldom a problem, but if you plan to participate in the annual Port Alberni Salmon Festival over the Labour Day weekend, book well in advance as this event is always well attended.

If your travelling companions are not interested in fishing, they won't be bored. Sproat Lake Provincial Park, located west of town, offers campsites, picnic sites, swimming, and trout fishing. Also on Sproat Lake they can see the only two Martin Mars aircraft remaining in the world. Built during the Second World War as troop carriers, these Coulson Flying Tankers have since been used to fight thousands of forest fires throughout western Canada and the USA and have earned an honourable reputation. The world's largest water bombers, they are capable of scooping up and carrying 6,000 gallons of water, which weighs over 27 tons.

Avid birders can visit the J.V. Cline Bird Sanctuary, which is an over-wintering ground for trumpeter swans. Some of your more energetic companions might also consider driving to Great Central Lake to take a guided kayak excursion or arrange for a cruise to the lake's far end and then hike the 22 kilometres to Della Falls, which at 1,443 feet is the highest waterfall in North America. Be warned, however, that it's the same distance back.

Those who simply wish to stroll around town at their leisure may visit the Alberni Valley Museum with its excellent displays of artifacts related to First Nations culture, the area's industrial history and local folk art. The Harbour Quay waterfront park and marketplace offers an interesting blend of art galleries, gift shops and restaurants, and for a truly interesting and memorable experience, at the 1912 CPR Station they may board the Alberni Pacific Railway train, which is pulled by a completely restored 1929 Baldwin logging locomotive. The track meanders through the city and surrounding forest, with stops at the Chase and Warren Winery for a tour and tasting and the McLean Mill National Historic Site. The only steam-operated sawmill in Canada, the McLean Mill cuts lumber for demonstrations and sale.

Alberni Inlet.

Restaurants range from typical fast food and small mom-and-pop eateries to ethnic and fine dining. Some are open 24 hours, and in addition to early morning breakfasts many can provide anglers with box lunches.

Those trailering their own boats will find that Clutesi Haven Marina has a 4-lane, all-tides ramp suitable for boats of all sizes. The single-lane ramp at Alberni Harbour Quay is best suited for small or shallow-draft boats. Although both usually have ample parking, overflow parking can usually be found reasonably close by. China Creek Park Marina and Campground, 14 km southwest of town, has a 4-lane, all-tides ramp that handles large boats and there is plenty of parking.

## Weather and Water Conditions

Alberni Inlet enjoys a moderate climate. Late fall and winter are typically West Coast wet, but spring and summer rains are infrequent and seldom long-lasting. Fog is more of a problem out near Barkley Sound, especially during July and August. The high mountains on each side of the Inlet offer summer-long protection from winds until the weather patterns change in mid- to late September. During July, August and early September the waters are fairly stable, but thermal drafts between midday and late afternoon can create uncomfortable conditions.

With no reefs, back eddies, tide rips or whirlpools, Alberni Inlet is classic small boat water where you might see everything from kayaks, tiny dinghies and inflatables up to houseboats, yachts and ocean-going cruisers. Most common, however, are 14- to 16-footers with suitable-sized outboards, which provide a good margin of safety and comfort and are easily manoeuvred when conditions get crowded. Many anglers fish the Inlet with neither electronics nor compass, but a depth sounder is advantageous.

## Run Timing

When it comes to salmon fishing, the names Alberni Inlet and Murphy are synonymous. It all started with Gordon Murphy,

David Murphy guided Pat Bates of Vancouver, BC, onto this trophy chinook. *Murphy Sportfishing photo*

former owner of Clutesi Haven Marina, who ranked as one the area's most popular and respected fishing guides. His love of fishing was passed on to his daughter Marilyn and son David, who both started guiding in their early teens. Gordon is now retired, but Marilyn and David are carrying on the family tradition with Murphy Sportfishing. Riverside Lodge, a huge, attractive-looking log structure overlooking the Stamp River, is their year-round operation that caters to both saltwater and freshwater anglers, while from June 1 to September 1, they operate in Kyuquot Sound with their land-based Murphy's Kyuquot Lodge and the *Daleanne*, a comfortable, 15-passenger motor vessel.

David Murphy says that migratory chinooks and coho begin arriving along the outskirts of Barkley Sound during June and then move closer inshore as the season progresses. By the first week in August, chinook vanguards have usually entered Alberni Inlet as far as Lone Tree Point, which starts a fishery that continues until mid-September. Coho tend to hold back in the inlet, but chinooks eventually move into Alberni Harbour where it shallows to about 80 feet. Active feeding ceases at this stage, but occasional fish—often of trophy proportions—can be antagonized into striking. These fish will continue massing until the first fall rains raise the river level and cool its temperature.

Sockeye also start showing in Barkley Sound during June but receive little attention from anglers who have eyes only for slab chinooks. Early sockeye run about 4 to 7 pounds but later fish average 8 pounds, with rare trophies up to 12 pounds. Sockeye become favoured targets around late June when they start entering Alberni Inlet. The season peaks during the first two weeks of July but continues until early August. Many anglers fish for chinooks in the morning then sockeye in the afternoon.

While coho arrive in Barkley Sound beginning in June, they don't usually start entering the Inlet in large numbers until late August. This is usually the best month for those interested in combining chinook, sockeye and coho fishing, but some dedicated chinook enthusiasts wait until September before hitting the Inlet. By this time the crowds have thinned out dramatically, and the chinooks are fully matured with some weighing over 50 pounds. Fishing generally remains good during the first two weeks of September, depending on the river's height and water temperature. Then as the chinook catches start dwindling, coho action is picking up and usually lasts well into October for fish to 20-plus pounds.

## Hotspots and Tactics

Weather permitting, by running out to the Barkley Sound feeding grounds, Port Alberni anglers can fish for feeder chinooks and bottom fish throughout the winter. Boats with enclosed cabins are recommended since staying reasonably warm and dry is the secret to enjoyable winter fishing. Your boat should also be outfitted with a full range of navigational equipment as you will be out of the Inlet's narrow confines.

During the summer-long fishery, crowded conditions are an accepted fact of life on Alberni Inlet. However, as long as everyone involved displays a little common sense and courtesy, aside from the occasional unforeseen incident, it usually works reasonably well. Whether targeting chinooks, sockeye or coho, downrigging is the preferred tactic because it provides precise depth control and allows several lines to be stacked at various levels on the cable. When everyone is using downriggers, a common trolling pattern evolves and then it's simply a matter of waiting for an opening where you can ease your boat into the procession. By following the established pattern and paying attention to what is going on around you, there should be room to manoeuvre your boat and avoid collisions. Inconsiderate anglers who ignore this basic rule usually end up in shouting matches after a hooked fish is lost because of a tangled or cut line. As the season

Robert Van Pelt had his hands full with this 40-pound chinook taken off Cous Creek in Alberni Inlet. He was using a hot pink Radiant FP Special hoochie trailed 28 inches behind a plaid Hot Spot flasher.

progresses and fishing effort increases, so unfortunately does the frequency of these noisy confrontations. Nevertheless, all things considered, it is a small price to pay for some truly memorable fishing experiences.

While sockeye favour both sides of the inlet, the eastern side often yields the best results all the way from Star Point on up to the harbour. On the western side, try from Nahmint Bay to Hocking Point and from Macktush Bay on past Dunsmuir Point to Cous Creek.

A boat trolling only one or two lines seldom has anywhere near the success as one with several lures in the water, so stack as many lines on the downrigger cable as you can handle. As a bare minimum, stack at least two lines about 15 feet apart on each downrigger cable, and for added flash try trailing a dummy flasher under the other gear on at least one cable. As the boat will be travelling very slowly, it is standard practice to leave the gear down while fish are played. As a school will keep following and striking the lures, multiple hook-ups are quite common.

As elsewhere along the West Coast, the "secret" to catching Alberni Inlet sockeye consists of using small lures, hoochies or flies and downrigging with them at dead-slow speeds in a fairly straight line. A typical rig consists of an O'Ki, Hot Spot or Gibbs flasher with orange or red trim and a small hoochie. Most popular are the Golden Bait MP16, MP15 and MP2 Mini-Plankton, Michael Bait MB182 and MB183, Angelo's Aquarium and Lady Luck. The leader length will depend on your boat speed—from 18 inches for slow to 27 inches for faster. Adjust leader lengths until you determine which works best for your boat's trolling speed.

Some anglers do well trolling with a small pink spoon behind a flasher. Two popular Coyote spoon patterns are the hot pink Nasty Boy and Halloween. Be warned that while fishing for sockeye it's not uncommon for large chinooks to intercept these tiny hoochies and spoons, but anglers who are fortunate enough to land them are never heard complaining.

A Golden Bait hoochie.

Black "oil slick" hoochie.

For early season chinooks and coho, start near the mouth of Alberni Inlet and then follow the action inward toward Alberni Harbour throughout the season. Bear in mind that a few areas inside the Inlet are closed to fishing, so consult the regulations and check with the DFO office in Port Alberni for any additional spot closures that might occur on short notice. Anglers with large, fast boats can start fishing between San Mateo Bay and Star Point, but most usually wait until the salmon move in closer, usually between Coleman Creek and Sproat Narrows. Except for the Nahmint Bay area, chinooks will generally favour the Inlet's right side until Cous Creek, just below Stamp Narrows.

One popular setup is a plaid Hot Spot flasher trailing a black "oil slick" hoochie, another is a gold Betsy O'Ki flasher with a Nasty Boy hoochie. Either flasher is also a good choice for trolling an anchovy in a Rhys Davis Anchovy Special in green, clear, or any of the metallic finishes.

David Murphy advises that the favourite hoochie colour for chinooks in the Inlet is red and that the leader lengths are critical—the faster the trolling speed the longer the leader. Start at 40 to 42 inches behind a flasher and then keep increasing the length until the fish turn on. At times this means going as long as can be managed while still permitting fish to be netted—up to 10 feet or so. However, avoid going longer than your rod because that makes netting your fish extremely difficult.

As they move farther inland, try Underwood Cove and the "China Creek Wall" between China Creek and Lone Tree Point at Stamp Narrows. From Cous Creek on, chinooks may be found pretty well anywhere inside the Inlet. A popular spot on the upper eastern side is the Boy Scout Camp south of Polly Point. Along the western shoreline try Stamp Point as well as mid-channel around Hohm, Hoik and Johnstone islands.

The annual Port Alberni Salmon Festival that traditionally ends on Labour Day will find hundreds of anglers gathering at familiar hotspots like Polly Point, Lone Tree Point, Pill Point, Kirby Point, Diplock Island and Swale Rock. There they will test their skills against big chinooks, which, if large enough, could generate up to $10,000 in prize money. The daily cash prizes are $3,000 for the largest salmon, $2,000 for the second largest, $1,000 for the third largest, and then some lucky angler pockets $7,000 for catching the largest salmon during the whole of this popular derby. In addition, there are daily hidden weight prizes.

When chinooks are staging in the upper Inlet, many anglers switch to trolling a large spoon like the Clendon Stewart and Wonder Spoon or various light-coloured plugs. It's not unusual to

Dave Boxrud's (right) winning chinook in the 2006 Port Alberni Salmon Festival weighed in at 44.6 pounds.

Peter Morrison's Chartreuse Clouser

see ancient models like carefully hoarded Alaskans, Lucky Louies and Wallace Highliners but most catches are made on Tomic plugs. Three that always seem to be in the winner's circle are no. 602 glow mother of pearl, 158 mother of pearl, and 900 gold. Whether using spoons or plugs, start at first light by trolling just a little under the surface, down say 10 to 20 feet, and as the day lightens gradually troll deeper until you are down 40 to 50 feet.

A warning: if you plan on trolling for chinooks with large plugs later in the season, consider 40-pound-test line minimum—better yet, 50-pound-test. Large plugs create drag that stretches nylon monofilament to its utmost so, when a large fish hits, there is little or no stretch left to act as a shock absorber and the line often breaks.

Expect the chinook fishery to last well past the middle of September, after which there should be good numbers of coho until mid-October or so. Some good spots for coho are usually out at Swale Rock, right in front of the Macktush Bay campsites and Bells Bay. Try a fast troll with an OAL12R hoochie, a Coyote, Tomic or Titan spoon without a flasher. If casting flies is your thing, standard favourites are Clouser Minnows or Lefty's Deceivers and variations of their many pretenders.

## AVAILABLE MARINE CHARTS

3668 Alberni Inlet

## Marine Chart Coordinates:

| Place Names: | | Place Names: | |
|---|---|---|---|
| Alberni Harbour | LAT 49°06' LONG 124°49' | Lone Tree Point | LAT 49°11' LONG 124°49' |
| Alberni Harbour Key | LAT 49°14' LONG 124°49' | Macktush Bay | LAT 49°07' LONG 124°50' |
| Alberni Inlet | LAT 49°05' LONG 124°50' | Nahmint Bay | LAT 49°04' LONG 124°52' |
| "Boy Scout Camp" | LAT 48°12' LONG 124°49' | Polly Point | LAT 49°13' LONG 124°49' |
| China Creek | LAT 49°09' LONG 124°48' | Port Alberni | LAT 49°14' LONG 124°48' |
| China Creek Marina | LAT 48°09' LONG 124°48' | River Point | LAT 49°06' LONG 124°49' |
| "China Creek Wall" | LAT 49°04' LONG 124°49' | San Mateo Bay | LAT 48°56' LONG 124°59' |
| Clutesi Haven Marina | LAT 49°16' LONG 125°03' | Somass River | LAT 49°14' LONG 124°49' |
| Coleman Creek | LAT 49°01' LONG 124°52' | Sproat Narrows | LAT 49°07' LONG 124°49' |
| Cous Creek | LAT 49°11' LONG 124°50' | Stamp Narrows | LAT 49°11' LONG 124°49' |
| Dunsmuir Point | LAT 49°09' LONG 124°48' | Stamp Point | LAT 49°13' LONG 124°50' |
| Hocking Point | LAT 49°05' LONG 124°50' | Star Point | LAT 48°58' LONG 124°57' |
| Hohm Island | LAT 49°14' LONG 124°50' | Ten Mile Point | LAT 49°04' LONG 124°50' |
| Hoik Island | LAT 49°14' LONG 124°50' | Underwood Cove | LAT 49°09' LONG 124°47' |
| Johnstone Island | LAT 49°15' LONG 124°49' | | |

The remote community of Bamfield is located amidst some of Vancouver Island's most spectacular scenery.

# Bamfield

Each summer the population of the tiny community of Bamfield, located near the southwest corner of Barkley Sound, swells from about 250 full-time residents to well over 1,000 as ocean kayakers, canoeists, scuba divers, nature watchers and West Coast Trail hikers swarm into the area. It is also a very popular destination from which to investigate what this vast saltwater angler's paradise has to offer. Visitors have five travel options for arriving in Bamfield: an airstrip on the outskirts of East Bamfield; the inlet, which is used by boats and floatplanes; the MV *Lady Rose*, a cargo and passenger vessel that sails from Port Alberni each Tuesday, Thursday and Saturday; Western Bus Lines, which operates out of Port Alberni from Monday through Friday; and their own vehicles via two gravel logging roads.

If you take the southern road route to Bamfield, you will follow Highway 18 from Duncan to Youbou then drive 85 km of gravel on

**Our Information Sources**

Doug Ferguson, Coastline Salmon Charters
Jeanne Ussher, Breaker's Marine

**For visitor information:**

BAMFIELD TOURIST/VISITOR INFO BOOTH
General Delivery
Bamfield, BC V0R 1B0
(250) 728-3006
lmyers@bamfield.ca
www.bamfieldcommunity.com

Central South Main. The eastern route is via Highway 19 or 19A to the Highway 4 junction and then, as you enter Port Alberni, you will take the south Port Alberni turnoff. From there it's about 102 km to Bamfield, with slightly over 80 km of that being Franklin Main and Sarita Main gravel roads. These are active logging roads so they are dusty and extremely rough in spots. Expect to meet large trucks, maintenance and service vehicles, plus plenty of local traffic. Frequent travellers in this area carry two spare tires for their vehicles and, if towing a trailer, two more for it.

Bamfield is actually two communities, one on either side of Bamfield Inlet. The road ends at East Bamfield, from which point travel to West Bamfield is by boat or water taxi. Prior to becoming accessible by road, the community was often referred to as "the Venice of the West Coast," and considering the important role that boats still play here, the name still seems quite appropriate.

According to Jeanne Ussher of Breaker's Marine, visitors will find a good range of accommodations that includes a half a dozen fishing lodges, an equal number of outfits offering cottages, several bed and breakfast operations, 3 campgrounds and a motel. If you book accommodations in West Bamfield, arrangements can be made for pickup at the government dock.

There are 4 government docks here, 2 on each side of the Inlet, and all become congested during the summer. Larger boats can be anchored or moored in Bamfield Inlet, Grappler Inlet and Port Desire. There is also an excellent public launch ramp at Port Desire, but the adjacent parking area fills to capacity during late July and August. Rental boats are available at Breaker's Marine, and there are several independent charter operations in the area.

Anglers arriving with their own boats for the first time should consider hiring a guide for at least their initial trip. Offshore fishing requires a fairly large, seaworthy boat equipped with standard safety equipment and the usual assortment of marine charts, compass, VHF radio, Global Positioning System and—for serious boaters—a radar unit. The easiest way to locate the offshore banks is to follow the regulars out in the morning and then stay with them; however, if it turns foggy and visibility plummets to near zero, you will require those navigation aids to get safely back to port.

## Weather and Water Conditions

After the rainy season starts in late September, the weather deteriorates until heavy winter rains and high winds make offshore fishing virtually impossible until late January. Even when feeder chinooks begin staging offshore during early February, the conditions out there, though more reasonable, are still unpredictable. Generally, most fishing occurs during early mornings when the water is calmest.

Expect some fog during the spring fishery and then lots of it as the weather warms. Fortunately, summer fogs usually burn off by noon. Summer weather is generally favourable but high swells are a fact of life on the open ocean. Always keep a sharp watch on weather and sea conditions for rapid changes.

## Run Timing

Doug Ferguson of Coastline Salmon Charters, who has been guiding in the Bamfield area since 1980, knows the area intimately and reports that while January and February are good for feeder chinooks, some of the best action starts in February when the herring spawning migration moves in around the northern shoreline of Barkley Sound. Chinooks range anywhere from sub-legal to 25 pounds but usually average in the high teens to low 20s with occasional fish into the 30s.

March and April find larger chinooks on the offshore banks as well as several areas inside Barkley Sound. After the herring spawn tapers off, usually by early April, inshore chinook fishing declines as the fish move back to the bait-rich banks offshore. By mid-May there are chinooks to 20-plus pounds around Kirby Point on Diana Island, Edward King Island, Bordelais Islets, Folger Island, Cape Beale and Keeha Bay. Mid-May should also see coho around Cree Island, located at the southeast corner of the Broken Group. These are followed at month's end by sockeye, which will start moving into Alberni Inlet about mid-June. The action continues offshore throughout June, but migratory chinooks, coho and sockeye that begin arriving along the outskirts of Barkley Sound during June move closer inshore as the season progresses.

July offers an excellent mixed bag of fishing in Barkley Sound for chinooks, coho and sockeye plus good offshore chinook action. With the exception of sockeye, inshore fishing continues good throughout August. By mid- to late September, migratory chinooks thin out, but coho action heats up until mid-October, weather permitting.

## Hotspots and Tactics

Fishing for feeder chinooks is fair to excellent all winter but expect lots of shakers early on. Weather permitting, January prospects range from slow to good around Cape Beale and the channel located right off the mouth of Bamfield Inlet. Also try around Diplock Island, Rainy Bay, Pill Point on Seddall Island, Vernon Bay and Swale Rock on the northeastern corner of the Broken Group.

Bob Guest with a 29-pound chinook taken at Pill Point near Bamfield. *Susanne Guest photo*

A typical setup for winter fishing is a green Stryper or plaid Hot Spot flasher trailing an anchovy in a Rhys Davis Anchovy Special attached to a 27- to 36-inch leader. If you prefer hoochies, try a blue baron or motorcycle pattern. Spoons are also an option, say a 5-inch Coyote in Nasty Boy, nickel neon blue or Halloween, with or without a flasher.

The action heats up in February when herring move in around Barkley Sound's northern shoreline. Locate the bait and you will find chinook action, often at depths of 40 to 90 feet. When chinook fishing slows as herring move back onto the banks, your best bets are the out-side reaches of Barkley Sound on the Bamfield side or the offshore banks themselves, some of which are located up to 40 km out on the open Pacific. Best known are La Pérouse (known locally as "Big Bank"), "Little Bank," "South Bank," "Lighthouse Bank" and "The Wreck." Baitfish congregate along the edges and down the sides of the banks, and chinooks are often found suspended at depths of 100 to 180 feet, occasionally down to 250 feet. These banks usually stop producing near the end of July when chinooks follow the bait inshore.

Chinook action continues in June around the Bamfield area, Rainy Bay, Vernon Bay, along the surf line and offshore. Sockeye start moving into Alberni Inlet and then the coho fishing picks up around Bamfield, Cree Island, Effingham Island, northward along the Broken Group to

Swale Rock and in Rainy Bay. By month's end coho to 9 pounds are possible off Cape Beale. Green Stryper and plaid flashers are still a good choice, but try a purple glow Anchovy Special with your anchovy or herring. It's worth noting that a gold 7-inch Tomic spoon has developed a great reputation for producing big chinooks in June.

Sockeye should now be showing up, but pretty well everyone will still be looking for big chinooks. If you want to catch some great fish for the barbecue, try just outside of Bamfield Harbour mouth, beside "The Wall" and along the back of Flemming Island. Try an 8-inch Hot Spot mini-flasher in silver Mylar or crushed pearl with a small hoochie on an 18- to 27-inch leader. The most popular patterns are Golden Bait MP16, MP15 and MP2 Mini Plankton, and Michael Bait MB182 and MB183.

Best bets for July are the Bamfield area, Cree Island, Kirby Point, "Little Bank" and "South Bank." Try the surf line, Cape Beale and Diplock Island for occasional coho to 12 pounds. Drift-jigging can be productive along the beach from Cape Beale to Roquefeuil Bay (known locally as "Kelp Bay"), especially along the steep drop-off between Whittlestone Point and Aguilar Point, past the mouth of Bamfield Inlet and on up to Roquefeuil Bay. While relating this information to us, Doug Ferguson of Coastline Salmon Charters mentioned that in 1984 he took his largest chinook to date, 54.5 pounds, about 100 feet off of Cape Beale on a Pirken and that four years later his best coho nailed a Stingsilda at the same spot. It weighed 24.3 pounds.

The entire western side of the Deer Group remains good throughout the summer. At the southwestern end in Hammond Passage, try the east side of Folger Island and Leach Islet and across the passage from Bordelais Islets northward along Edward King Island, past the entrance of Dodger Channel, and from Kirby Point to Sandford Island. Near the top end of the Deer Group, try from the sheer drop-off along the north side of Diplock Island over to Gattie Point and then to the east side of Weld Island. Drift-jigging is popular around the Deer Group throughout the summer and often proves more productive than trolling. This involves fishing in close to rock piles and islands where ocean swells create powerful wave surges. This is not recommended for inexperienced or inattentive boat handlers or for those in boats with balky motors.

August is excellent for chinooks from Cape Beale to the mouth of Alberni Inlet, with much of the best action still close in around

A pink bucktail is often a good choice
early in the season.

Bamfield. Coho are best off
Cape Beale and the surf line.
The accepted procedure at Cape
Beale is for boats to line up and take turns fishing along the edge of the
breakers—but only when it's your turn. Good fishing manners are
mandatory. And prepare your tackle beforehand because, with so many
boats manoeuvring in close quarters, there is no time to think about rigging rods or tying knots.

Rainy Bay is prime for big chinooks from August until as late as mid-
September, depending on when the first autumn rains attract them into
Alberni Inlet. Try from the deep west arm around to the south side of
the Boyson Islands and along either side of Chup Point. Two other traditional August hotspots are Swale Rock and Kirby Point.

By early September there are some excellent opportunities for chinooks to 40-plus pounds off Whittlestone Point, Cape Beale, "The
Wall," Kirby Point and Robbers Passage. Your chances for coho to 12-
plus pounds are much improved, especially around Brady Beach, the
back of Flemming Island and in Satellite Passage.

Anchovy is still the heavy favourite with most chinook anglers, but
those after coho often opt for hoochies like a motorcycle, blue baron or
purple haze. This is a great time to try bucktailing or skip-fly fishing on
the surface, and fly fishers can do well casting various sizes and colours
of Clouser Minnows and Deceivers. Coho are quite picky at times, their
preference depending on which food source they happen to be targeting. During early morning low-light conditions try a pink/white fly,
then during the daylight hours experiment with purple/white,
green/white or blue/white in lengths of 2½ to 5 inches.

## AVAILABLE MARINE CHARTS

3671 Barkley Sound
3602 Juan de Fuca Strait, Approaches
3646 Bamfield Inlet
3668 Alberni Inlet
3670 Broken Group

## Marine Chart Coordinates:

| Place Names: | | Place Names: | |
|---|---|---|---|
| Aguilar Point | LAT 48°50' LONG 125°08' | Hammond Passage | LAT 48°50' LONG 125°14' |
| Alberni Inlet | LAT 49°05' LONG 124°50' | Imperial Eagle Channel | LAT 48°54' LONG 125°12' |
| Bamfield | LAT 48°50' LONG 125°08' | Kirby Point | LAT 48°51' LONG 125°13' |
| Bamfield Inlet | LAT 48°49' LONG 125°08' | La Pérouse Bank (Big Bank) | LAT 48°45' LONG 125°55' |
| Barkley Sound | LAT 48°51' LONG 125°23' | Lawton Point | LAT 48°48' LONG 125°11' |
| Bordelais Islets | LAT 48°49' LONG 125°14' | Leach Islet | LAT 48°50' LONG 125°14' |
| Boyson Islands | LAT 48°58' LONG 125°02' | Lighthouse Bank | LAT 48°52' LONG 125°38' |
| Brady Beach | LAT 48°50' LONG 125°09' | Pill Point | LAT 48°58' LONG 125°05' |
| Broken Group | LAT 48°54' LONG 125°20' | Rainy Bay | LAT 48°58' LONG 125°02 |
| Cape Beale | LAT 48°47' LONG 125°13' | Robbers Passage | LAT 48°54' LONG 125°07' |
| Chup Point | LAT 48°57' LONG 125°02' | Roquefeuil Bay (Kelp Bay) | LAT 48°52' LONG 125°07' |
| Cree Island | LAT 48°51' LONG 125°20' | Sandford Island | LAT 48°52' LONG 125°10' |
| Deer Group | LAT 48°51' LONG 125°11' | Satellite Passage | LAT 48°52' LONG 125°11' |
| Diana Island | LAT 48°51' LONG 125°11' | Seddall Island | LAT 48°58' LONG 125°04' |
| Diplock Island | LAT 48°56' LONG 125°07' | South Bank | LAT 48°50' LONG 125°49' |
| Dodger Channel | LAT 48°51' LONG 125°12' | Swale Rock | LAT 48°55' LONG 125°13' |
| Edward King Island | LAT 48°50' LONG 125°12' | Tapaltos Bay | LAT 48°48' LONG 126°11' |
| Effingham Island | LAT 48°52' LONG 125°19' | "The Wreck" | LAT 48°44' LONG 125°53' |
| Flemming Island | LAT 48°53' LONG 125°08' | Vernon Bay | LAT 48°59' LONG 125°09' |
| Folger Island | LAT 48°50' LONG 125°15' | Weld Island | LAT 48°57' LONG 125°05' |
| Gattie Point | LAT 48°56' LONG 125°05' | Whittlestone Point | LAT 48°49' LONG 125°11' |

# Port Renfrew

Port Renfrew is located 72 km west of Sooke on Highway 14, a narrow road that winds through logged-over areas in various stages of regrowth and overlooks several beautiful ocean vistas. Although the community is small—population about 400—the range of accommodations includes several bed and breakfast operations, 2 motels, a hotel, cabins, and 3 campgrounds with RV parks. The well-stocked Port Renfrew General Store has a full line of groceries and also operates as a liquor outlet. For dining check out the Lighthouse Pub and Restaurant and the Port Renfrew Hotel and Pub.

In addition to saltwater fishing, visitors may indulge in ocean kayaking, canoeing on the San Juan River, fishing in nearby rivers and lakes, and even hiking on the world-famous West Coast Trail that begins at Port Renfrew. Most visitors plan at least one trip to nearby Botanical Beach where steep sandstone cliffs are part of spectacular landscapes that tempt even the most jaded scenic photographers. At their base, tidal pools contain intriguing formations that have been sculpted and shaped into the soft sandstone by waves tumbling much harder rocks against it. An abundance of intertidal life is to be found here, including virtually thousands of species of plants and animals—crabs, clams,

## Our Information Sources

Elliot Williams, fishing guide, Port
Renfrew

## For visitor information:

SOOKE VISITOR CENTRE
Box 774
2070 Phillips Road
Sooke, BC V0S 1N0
(250) 642-7089
info@sooke.museum.bc.ca
www.sooke.museum.bc.ca

starfish, chitons, anemones, barnacles, snails, mussels and sea urchins—that have adapted to conditions that vary from hard-pounding surf to lengthy dry periods.

If you are interested in a guided fishing trip, there are over a dozen fishing charter businesses in the area. Be warned, however, that the charter operators are often booked solid during peak periods, so booking in advance is recommended. If towing your own boat, you will find launch ramps and moorage at the Port Renfrew Marina and the Pacheedaht First Nation Campground and RV Park.

As fishing out of Port Renfrew takes place on the open Pacific and often involves running 35 to 40 km offshore to Swiftsure Bank, it is no place for a poorly equipped boat or an inexperienced operator. A fully equipped, seaworthy boat is an absolute must as is knowledge and experience about navigation and boat handling in adverse sea conditions. The stretch between Bamfield and Port Renfrew is known as the "Graveyard of the Pacific" because there are few places to go ashore during calm weather—and none at all when it's rough. Many anglers very wisely use the buddy system while fishing offshore and head out in groups of two or more boats.

## Swiftsure Bank's Closed Area

Those planning to fish on Swiftsure Bank in Management Area 121 should first familiarize themselves with the portion that has been permanently closed to recreational and commercial fishing since 1992. The affected area lies inside a line from 48°34.00'N and 125°06.00'W, thence to 48°34.00'N and 124°54.20'W, thence to 48°29.62'N and 124°43.40'W, thence following the International Boundary between Canada and the US to 48°29.55'N and 124°56.20'W and thence in a straight line to the point of commencement. This area is closed to fishing for all finfish all year.

Fishing in a closed area is a serious violation of the law and persons so doing should be reported to the toll-free line at 1-800-465-4336.

Calm water conditions mean fast runs can be made out to Swiftsure Bank.

## Weather and Water Conditions

As elsewhere along the Island's west coast there are frequent storms during late fall, winter and early spring, and generally by November the stormy weather has made saltwater fishing virtually impossible. Occasional calm days during the winter might permit getting out there but seldom very far offshore. The prevailing winter winds are usually southeasters.

During the rest of the year low-pressure systems generally result in fairly calm, warmer weather—albeit damp—and prevailing summer winds are usually southwesters. Mornings offer the calmest water conditions. Expect fog from June to September but it usually burns off by midday.

Port Renfrew is at the southern extreme of Vancouver Island's rain forest and the average annual rainfall is 145 inches, so go prepared with suitable clothing. If you are chartering, you will find that almost all of the guides provide rain clothing but check beforehand just to make sure.

## Run Timing

This forage-rich area is one of the major feeding grounds for juvenile chinooks and coho on the Island's west coast. As many salmon are local stocks from the Nitinat and San Juan rivers, they are robust and often somewhat larger than the average feeder chinooks found elsewhere.

At varying times between February and May vast schools of herring migrate inshore to the kelp beds to spawn, creating an outstanding mixed-bag fishery for feeder chinooks and halibut. This action continues until the herring head back offshore after spawning, at which time the chinook fishing around Swiftsure Bank picks up again.

The inshore fishing turns back on during early to mid-May with the appearance of the first of several waves of southward-migrating chinooks. These stocky, deep-bodied fish have long been touted as the "Columbia River" run, but many actually head for the Fraser River and its tributaries. While a high percentage of them weigh in the low to mid-20s, this is probably your best chance of catching a chinook weighing 30 to 40 pounds, with occasional trophies reported at 50-plus pounds. This run peaks around late June but a few big chinooks continue showing up right through August, by which time they are somewhat longer and more slender for their weight.

Migrating sockeye and pinks provide good fishing from late July through August, with odd-year pink salmon abundance quickly producing limit catches for those who are so inclined. The runs of both species are pretty well over by the end of August, but by that time increasing numbers of returning Robertson Creek and Nitinat River chinooks are showing up in the catches, followed by San Juan River stocks.

July through September should see increasing numbers of coho passing by, and then chums start in late August and continue well into October along with late-running northern coho, many headed for the San Juan River. Each season sees chums and northern coho weighing 20-plus pounds weighed in at the marinas.

## Hotspots and Tactics

Feeder chinooks are present all winter in this area, so it's mainly a matter of waiting for suitable weather conditions in order to try for them. Downrigging with an anchovy behind a flasher is the standard operating procedure, but some anglers prefer plugs and/or spoons. The most productive action head colours usually incorporate blues and greens, so experiment with these two colours in clear and glow along with chrome blue/green and chrome green/chartreuse.

Depending on the time of year, feeder chinook (and halibut) fishing is either close inshore or else offshore on Swiftsure Bank, but the other four salmon species may be found virtually anywhere between these two places while they are on their southward migrations. This is when large schools of coho are usually found feeding somewhere between Swiftsure Bank and Port Renfrew—but locating them is the trick. The accepted procedure is to simply monitor your VHF radio to determine where the action is. At other times coho are so thick out on Swiftsure that it's almost impossible to get a bait or lure down through them in order to fish for chinooks.

When herring migrate inshore to spawn on the kelp beds between Owen Point and Nitinat Narrows, anglers can fish for feeder chinooks and halibut at the same time by downrigging or motor-mooching. For the former try a red or green/silver Mylar Hot Spot flasher trailing a large anchovy in a Rhys Davis Anchovy Special or an O'Ki Juan de Fuca Head on a 50- to 72-inch leader. If anchovies aren't available, try a Tyee strip. For motor-mooching, use a 6- to 8-inch-long cut-plug herring on a 6- to 10-foot leader behind a 6- to 8-ounce sinker. Although feeder chinooks elsewhere generally prefer cut-plugs with a slow roll, some regulars fishing these inshore waters modify the angles to produce a faster roll.

Good inshore areas to prospect include the outer reaches of Port San Juan, especially between Owen Point and Camper Bay where a ledge that closely borders the shoreline averages about 12 to 18 metres deep. Watch for a shallow reef that juts up almost vertically just off Owen Point; it is festooned with cannonballs left by anglers who didn't! This is also a good area later on in the season when the migratory chinooks appear as they are usually to be found feeding right in close along the kelp beds. Coho tend to stay farther out.

As herring head back offshore after spawning, feeder chinook fishing picks up again around Swiftsure Bank. Anchovy is definitely the bait of choice, with a whole herring of suitable size the runner-up. Use either with a Rhys Davis Anchovy Special trailed 50 to 72 inches behind a red Stryper or glow-in-the-dark Hot Spot flasher.

Plugs are an option at times here, but as they should match the bait in size, you will need a selection from 4 to 7 inches long. Popular Tomic models include the no. 55, 158, 232, 301, 500, 602, and 700. For spoons, keep that preference for blues and greens in mind and consider the Coyote in nickel/neon blue, nickel/neon green and glo green or Tomics in no. 238, 403, 632G and 774.

When the migratory coho show up, stick with the blues and greens when choosing hoochies or squirts and shorten the leader to 42 inches. The same spoons will also work but to them add a few Tom Macks in nickel and 50/50 brass/nickel. This is also a great time for drift-jigging with Buzz Bombs, Pirkens, Stingsildas and Zzingers. Matching the bait's size is usually more important than the lure colour, but favour those that incorporate blue or green in their pattern. For pink and sockeye salmon try a small, sparse hoochie in varying shades of red, pink or orange trailing 18 to 24 inches behind a red crushed pearl Hot Spot mini-flasher.

Later in the season try downrigging for inshore northern coho with a cut-plug herring without a flasher or motor-mooch with a 6- to 8-ounce sinker. The same tactics work for chums, but you will probably do better with an anchovy in an action head. Once you locate the action, you may want to switch to drift-jigging.

## AVAILABLE MARINE CHARTS

3602 Approaches to Juan de Fuca Strait
3606 Juan de Fuca
3647 Port San Juan and Nitinat River

## Marine Chart Coordinates:

| Place Names: | | Place Names: | |
|---|---|---|---|
| Bamfield | LAT 48°50' LONG 125°08' | Owen Island | LAT 48°33' LONG 124°30' |
| Bonilla Point | LAT 48°36' LONG 124°43' | Owen Point | LAT 48°33' LONG 124°30 |
| Botanical Beach | LAT 48°32' LONG 124°26' | Port Renfrew | LAT 48°33' LONG 124°25' |
| Camper Bay | LAT 48°33' LONG 124°33' | Port San Juan | LAT 48°33' LONG 124°27' |
| Carmanah Point | LAT 48°37' LONG 124°45' | Providence Cove | LAT 48°31' LONG 124°24' |
| Cerantes Rock | LAT 48°32' LONG 124°28' | Quartertide Rocks | LAT 48°33' LONG 124°28' |
| Clo-oose | LAT 48°39' LONG 124°49' | San Juan Point | LAT 48°32' LONG 124°27' |
| Cullite Cove | LAT 48°34' LONG 124°36' | San Juan River | LAT 48°34' LONG 124°24' |
| Gordon River | LAT 48°35' LONG 124°25' | Sooke | LAT 48°23' LONG 123°43' |
| Hammond Rocks | LAT 48°32' LONG 124°27' | Swiftsure Bank | LAT 48°34' LONG 124°59' |
| Kellet Rock | LAT 48°32' LONG 124°29' | Thrasher Cove | LAT 48°33' LONG 124°28' |
| Nitinat Narrows | LAT 48°40' LONG 124°51' | Wallbran Creek | LAT 48°35' LONG 124°40' |

# Sooke

One of the oldest settlements on Vancouver Island's west coast, Sooke is ideally located for recreational fishing. About 35 km west of Victoria, this growing community includes Saseenos, Sooke, and East Sooke, all bordering the Sooke Basin and Sooke Harbour. Accommodations range from a provincial campground to the world-famous Sooke Harbour House. There are also about 20 operations offering cottages for rent, 30 bed and breakfasts, and 3 campgrounds. Sunny Shores Resort and Marina, 5621 Sooke Road, offers a motel, an RV/tent campground, a launch ramp, moorage, boat rentals, and a fuel dock. Jock's Dock and

Sunny Shores Resort and Marina in Sooke Harbour offers a launch ramp, moorage, boat rentals and a fuel dock.

Crab Shack, 6947 West Coast Road, has a launch ramp, but if there is less than a 2-foot tide, you will probably experience trouble with anything except small boats. The Crab Shack is a great place to purchase live crabs and other fresh and frozen seafood. The Sooke Harbour Authority, also located in Sooke Harbour, offers moorage, and Vacations West Resort Motel has 120 berths.

## Weather and Water Conditions

Sooke enjoys a moderate climate with most rainfall confined to the relatively mild winter months. Summers are generally pleasant but taking along wet weather clothing is recommended. The prevailing westerly winds can be troublemakers but early mornings frequently offer calm water. Conditions can worsen on warm days when thermal winds meet cooler ocean air, usually about midday. Depending on the location, tides can run about 5 to 18 km/h but seldom form big eddies or rips.

### Our Information Sources

Mark Grant, owner, Mark Grant's Charters
Brian Lacroix, owner, Brian Lacroix Salmon Charters
Rod Sullivan, owner, Saltwater Salmon Charters

### For visitor information:

SOOKE VISITOR CENTRE
Box 774
2070 Phillips Road
Sooke, BC V0S 1N0
(250) 642-7089
info@sooke.museum.bc.ca
www.sooke.museum.bc.ca

Brian Lacroix has fished this area extensively for over 20 years but didn't start chartering until 2004. He advises that the tidal currents run east and west at average speeds from undetectable to about 6 km/h. An 18-km/h easterly or westerly wind with a contradicting 5-km/h tide can create dangerous water conditions. A good source of wind information is www.bigwavedave.ca, and Lacroix urges all boaters to use it before heading out. "The wind can come up extremely fast," he adds, "and those who are unaware of forecasts and tend to push it, often get into trouble."

Both harbour and basin are well protected from offshore winds, but the mouth of Sooke Harbour (Sooke Bluffs) has dissimilar tides to those in Juan de Fuca Strait. The waters in the harbour ebbing while the Strait is flooding creates very unstable conditions from Possession Point past the west end of the Bluffs. If a westerly or easterly wind happens to come up, this area becomes extremely dangerous and you might have real problems trying to re-enter Sooke Harbour.

Tide changes are favoured fishing times as they often trigger salmon feeding binges; however, mid-morning tide changes mixed with brisk westerlies can make for rough water conditions. Another problem anglers face during the summer fishery is the presence of salmon-eating killer whales, which may put off the bite for two or three hours. But if the orcas happen to be seal- and sea-lion eaters, the salmon seem to know this and there is no impact on the bite.

## Run Timing

Good year-round fishing starts immediately beyond Whiffen Spit on the open waters of Juan de Fuca Strait. There are excellent numbers of winter chinooks, possibly the longest-lasting runs of big migratory chinooks on the entire West Coast, runs of coho, sockeye and chum that vary in abundance and timing, some outstanding pink salmon action during the odd years, and bottom fishing opportunities that include halibut to 200-plus pounds.

Winter chinook fishing starts in late October with fish averaging 4 to 12 pounds though occasionally running to 20 pounds. Somewhat larger feeder chinooks appear in late April and the fishing moves closer inshore. Good bets are a hoochie trailed behind a flasher, an anchovy behind a flasher or dodger, or a large herring strip fished with only an action head.

About mid-May big migratory "Columbia" chinooks move in,

though most of them will actually head for systems draining into the Strait of Georgia and the Fraser River. While the average chinook won't match the heavyweights of 60-plus pounds caught at other popular salt-water destinations, the sheer abundance of salmon in the 20- to 50-pound range more than makes up for this. Of equal importance is that, being on a major migration route, the number of these large chinooks that stop to feed before continuing their migrations provides a much longer fishing season than most other destinations enjoy. One need only consider the abundance of forage available in the area to determine why it attracts and holds migrating salmon. Included on the menu are herring, anchovies, needlefish (sand lance), pilchards (sardines), shrimp, squid, and periodic crab hatches.

The average migratory chinooks will weigh in the low to mid-20s, with early June the best time for a 50-pounder. The run peaks about the last two weeks of June but a few heavyweights will also show up in late August. Occasional fish in the 60-pound class are reported but these are rare.

The coho situation has been so disrupted and unreliable in recent years that attempting to suggest possible abundance levels and run times creates confusion for everyone involved. In "the good old days" resident bluebacks (immature coho) were present throughout the winter, often in numbers that created a real nuisance for anglers fishing for winter chinooks. These juvenile stocks are no longer present and whether they will ever become re-established remains to be seen.

A small run of migratory coho that average 4 to 6 pounds might appear from late June to mid-July, but the timing of once dependable coho runs past the area is also a thing of the past. Some years the numbers have been so depressed that total coho closures were imposed. Later season coho are usually present from late August through September and some northern coho appear in October. These fish range from 3 pounds to the high teens but average 6 to 12 pounds. These late runs have a tendency to swim deeper than normal, often from 75 to 120 feet.

Sockeye start appearing in early July and remain in the area until August. Although they are taken fairly close to shore, most of the action is offshore around the second to fourth tide lines, well out—up to 8 km—in the shipping lanes. Be extra careful if there is fog as those big ocean-going ships move surprisingly fast. For this very reason, having radar and a radar reflector on your boat is recommended.

During their odd-year peak cycle, pink salmon show up in abundance from early to mid-July until the end of September.

As chinook fishing slows during early August, coho and pinks continue arriving and then a second wave of chinooks appears. Anglers then have a choice of fishing close to shore for chinooks or heading offshore to the tide lines for coho and pinks.

There is usually a big run of chums late in the season, many heading for the Sooke River, but relatively few anglers bother with them. Those who do are often rewarded with some memorable days for these are strong, rambunctious fish that test the strength of tackle and abilities of the anglers. They average 10 to 15 pounds but 20-pounders are taken every year. They are usually in the top 60 feet of water and readily take anchovies.

## Hotspots and Tactics

Popular spots between Sooke and Victoria that frequently produce good catches include right in front of the Sooke Harbour entrance along to Sooke Bluffs, Possession Point, Secretary Island, O'Brien Point and the "Trap Shack." Productive areas in June are Otter Point and northwest along Gordons Beach to Sheringham Point. Not many anglers fish for salmon past Sheringham, but Point No Point can be good at times and, because it is fairly remote, you won't have to worry about crowded

Matt Payne of Victoria with a typical feeder chinook from the Sooke area.

conditions. However, weather is a serious consideration if you plan to go that far because once past Otter Point there isn't anywhere handy to put in if water conditions turn nasty.

The "Trap Shack" is so named from the days when fish traps were established at various points along the shoreline. The two most productive ones were located at Possession Point and Cabin Point, which is a bit past the midway point between Possession Point and Beechey Head. The "Trap Shack" is a favourite from April through June but remains fairly popular right through until October. There are three reefs in this area, so check your marine chart beforehand to determine their location. Trolling by these reefs and in close to shore can be productive, especially during an ebb tide. Also worth a try for chinooks is farther out along the tide lines from the "Trap Shack" westward to Secretary Island.

Virtually everyone uses downriggers for the big chinooks and, while flashers are most predominant, there are times during June when dodgers are quite productive. Although increasing numbers of anglers are experimenting with bright-coloured hoochies, probably 90 percent of the fish are still taken on anchovies, whole herring or herring strip. When big chinooks arrive in the spring, try an anchovy 50 to 72 inches behind a red-trimmed green Hot Spot, O'Ki or Gibbs flasher. Recommended action heads include Krippled Anchovy, O'Ki JDF, and Rhys Davis Anchovy Special in clear, green, glow, purple haze, watermelon, bloody nose, mint pearl, and chrome purple/black.

Although anglers with smaller boats usually stay closer to their launching or mooring sites, those with fast, seaworthy boats often run from the Victoria waterfront to Otter Point for a morning of fishing, a run that takes up to 45 minutes if the water is calm. However, long runs like this are not required as much of the fishing is basically right along the shoreline and off the various points. If heading out of Sooke Harbour, for example, you have the option of going southeast to Beechey Head where there is good fishing although, because it is close to the Victoria waterfront, more competition.

Try downrigging close to the bottom along the 18- to 40-metre ledges. Popular baits for this are whole herring, herring strip, or an anchovy in a Rhys Davis Anchovy Special or an O'Ki Juan de Fuca. Hoochies in colours and sizes to match those of the squid or shrimp that are present are also good choices. Flashers are more popular than dodgers, with glow-in-the-dark finishes preferred by most anglers.

The accepted norm for sockeye and pink salmon is to use small pink, red or orange lures or hoochies behind a small silver or pearlescent white flasher trimmed with pink, red or orange. Brian Lacroix advises that, whenever targeting sockeye, to keep one line close to the surface. Although some anglers stick with downriggers while offshore, they shorten their leaders to 18 to 24 inches so the lures work faster. Many switch to flatline trolling with sinkers ranging from 2 to 8 ounces and run lures about 30 to 60 feet behind the boat. It is not uncommon to hook coho on lures and hoochies meant for sockeye and pinks, but you can hedge your bets by running a green/white hoochie behind one flasher.

Other anglers, meanwhile, do quite well on chinooks, coho and pinks by casting lures from rocky points and beaches. Gordons Beach is one such popular location. As the water there is quite shallow, avoid using heavy drift-jigs in favour of somewhat lighter spoons like Krocodiles, Gators and Deadly Dicks. As large chinooks are occasionally hooked from the beach, ensure that your reel has a good 200 yards minimum capacity—or better yet 300 yards.

By mid-September anglers are fishing the tail end of the pink run but the coho run is building. By the end of September coho fishing is usually good and some winter chinooks have started showing up. Try trolling from the large reef off the south side of Secretary Island out to the shipping lanes, but be aware that tide rips might drag you along in their current. The north side of Secretary—referred to as "The Gap"— has a reef off the island and another off Possession Point, which can make for tricky downrigging. Also bear in mind that this area is best avoided during rough water conditions.

There is a reef off the south side of Possession Point, another off the west side, and several pinnacles farther out that rise from 100 feet to 60 feet from the surface. Located between Possession Point and the mouth of Sooke Harbour is a very dangerous unmarked rock that is only visible during lower tides. As it can't be seen at all during higher tides, check your marine chart.

A Gibbs Gator spoon is a good choice for casting from beaches.

West of Possession Point, the Sooke Bluffs are relatively flat and have lots of kelp beds. This is the general area where the Juan De Fuca currents meet with Sooke Harbour tides, which can produce great fishing but also some very rough water conditions.

There are quite a few harbour seals in the area encompassing Secretary Island, Possession Point and Sooke Bluffs, and they are notorious for grabbing hooked salmon. When they become a problem, think about heading down toward the "Trap Shack" or up toward Otter Point where there are fewer of these pests. Otter Point is considered the safest and most popular place to fish. The only reef is right off the point and there are no other surprises. Baitfish get pushed in close to the shoreline in this area and they attract chinooks, especially during floods and ebbs. Troll along the wall to Gordons Beach but watch the current in close to the point or you might find yourself trolling backwards.

Brian Lacroix suggests that anglers can learn a lot about this productive area by simply driving to Otter Point and walking out to the point to observe how floods and ebbs create riptides that filter out into the strait. Although fishing them can be very productive, he cautions that a boat travelling against a riptide might be hardly moving or in some cases travelling backwards, while a boat running with the riptide will be virtually smoking along (trolling speed plus the current speed). Not paying attention in these cases can result in monumental line tangles, lost fish, flared tempers and much loud, abusive language.

Between Otter Point and Sheringham Point is Orveas Bay—though most locals refer to it as Muir Creek because that is the creek flowing into the bay at its midway point. The dense kelp beds here hold a lot of baitfish, which tend to attract more chinooks than other salmon species, but there is a drop-off from 12 to 48 metres along there, so monitor your depth sounder closely to prevent hanging up.

There are dangerous rocks and reefs at Sheringham Point—right in front of the lighthouse and to the west—that are exposed at the lower tides so you should always be aware of them. Sheringham is usually the least crowded place to fish, but even it can turn on if word of good fishing gets out. Some anglers favour it because it gives them the first crack at new runs as they arrive. However, Brian Lacroix points out that, when fishing at Sheringham Point, you are about 15 km from Sooke Harbour mouth, so if an easterly wind starts coming up, it's time to make tracks for home—*now*, not later.

## AVAILABLE MARINE CHARTS

3461 Juan de Fuca Strait, Eastern Portion
3462 Juan de Fuca Strait to Strait of Georgia
3641 Albert Head to Otter Point

### Marine Chart Coordinates:

| Place Names: | | Place Names: | |
|---|---|---|---|
| Becher Bay | LAT 48°20' LONG 123°37' | Saseenos | LAT 48°23' LONG 123°40' |
| Beechey Head | LAT 48°19' LONG 123°39' | Sheringham Point | LAT 48°23' LONG 123°55' |
| Donaldson (Secretary) Island | LAT 48°20' LONG 123°42' | Sooke | LAT 48°23' LONG 123°43' |
| East Sooke | LAT 48°22' LONG 123°41' | Sooke Basin | LAT 48°23' LONG 123°40' |
| Gordons Beach | LAT 48°22' LONG 123°50' | Sooke Bluffs | LAT 48°21' LONG 123°45' |
| O'Brien Point | LAT 48°20' LONG 123°42' | Sooke Harbour | LAT 48°22' LONG 123°43' |
| Otter Point | LAT 48°21' LONG 123°49' | Sooke Inlet | LAT 48°21' LONG 123°43' |
| Point No Point | LAT 48°23' LONG 123°59' | "Trap Shack" | LAT 48°19' LONG 123°41' |
| Possession Point | LAT 48°20' LONG 123°43' | Whiffen Spit | LAT 48°21' LONG 123°45' |

# Victoria

Vancouver Island's largest city is ideal for visiting anglers whose families or travelling companions are not enamoured with fishing. There is so much to see and do in this cosmopolitan city they should have no trouble keeping themselves amused and entertained while those smitten with the fishing bug are out on the water chasing dreams.

The City of Victoria has a population of approximately 74,100, but "Greater Victoria," which encompasses the 13 surrounding municipalities, exceeds 335,000 residents. It is a unique blend of genteel, laid-back quaintness and vibrant, ultramodern urbanity. The British influence of downtown Victoria becomes obvious by the presence of the provincial Parliament Buildings, Fairmont Empress Hotel, Christ Church Cathedral, the Royal London Wax Museum, and various English-style restaurants and pubs. Also located in the city centre is the oldest and most intact Chinatown in Canada, and those interested in the history of the region's original residents may spend hours viewing aboriginal exhibits at the acclaimed Royal British Columbia Museum.

Noted for its mild climate, year-round golfing at world-class courses, and its large population of retirees, Victoria is known for its easy-going pace of life. Add to these attractions the several urban lakes that contain healthy stocks of rainbow and cutthroat trout—even smallmouth and largemouth bass in a few of them—plus saltwater fishing opportunities for all five species of Pacific salmon and some truly humungous halibut, and it's easy to understand why Victoria is such a popular vacation destination for those who don't live there—but wish they did.

**Our Information Sources**

Sean Moore, former manager of Pedder Bay Marina and RV Park
Tom Vaida, fishing reporter, Island Outfitters Sportfishing Centre

As Victoria is popular with the sailing and boating set, there are two large marinas in the area but only a few launch ramps. Two of them are located at Uplands Park (Cattle Point), one on each side of the point; the James Bay Anglers' Association ramp is located at 75 Dallas Road and another ramp is at the Pedder Bay Marina at 925 Pedder Bay Drive in Metchosin, southwest of the city.

**For visitor information:**

VICTORIA VISITOR CENTRE
812 Wharf Street
Victoria, BC V8W 1T3
Tel: (250) 953-2033
info@tourismvictoria.com
www.tourismvictoria.com

## Weather and Water Conditions

Victoria experiences much lower rainfall than any other place on the BC coast. It owes this happy condition to the rain shadow effect created by the Olympic Mountains, located across the Strait of Juan de Fuca in Washington State. The average annual precipitation is 24 inches. By comparison, Seattle, 137 km to the southeast, receives 38 inches, and Vancouver, 100 km north, 48 inches. And just 80 km west of Victoria

"Barn door" halibut are often weighed in at Victoria area marinas.
*Reel Obsession Sport Fishing photo*

at Port Renfrew, the average annual rainfall is 145 inches. Almost two-thirds of Victoria's annual precipitation falls between November and February. During the summer months it is the driest major city in Canada, but this doesn't mean that you shouldn't take rain clothing along during the summer—you know, just in case.

Northeasters and southeasters are the prevailing winter winds, with northeasters usually the worst. Summer winds are generally westerlies or southwesters; a southeaster often results in bad conditions on the water. However, even on virtually windless summer days, thermal winds occur as the day warms up, usually from noon until 2 p.m., creating lumpy water until it eases off around 6 p.m. As most areas remain fairly calm during the mornings, many anglers plan on a morning and evening fishery, depending on the tides.

## Run Timing

Tom Vaida moved to Victoria in 1972 and started right in fishing. After joining the Clover Point Anglers' Association in 1993, he took up salmon fishing and has since devoted 30 to 40 days to it each season off the Victoria waterfront. Having written the weekly "South Island Fishing Report" for the Island Outfitter Sportfishing Centre since 1998, Tom is always well up on everything from weather conditions to where the fish are and what they are taking. According to him, large numbers of juvenile chinooks remain in Juan de Fuca Strait to feed on the

abundance of forage fish like herring, needlefish, anchovies and pilchards, plus squid, shrimp, prawns and crabs. Depending on their year class, these salmon range in size from sub-legal "shakers" up to 30-plus pounds. As spring progresses, the chinooks keep getting larger and by June they account for much of the effort,

Outdoor writer Tom Vaida with chinooks of 15 and 34 pounds taken while downrigging just off the Victoria Breakwater.

although halibut anglers are also watching the tides closely.

Weather permitting, after the January halibut closure is over, many anglers start downrigging close to the bottom with bait or lures that attract both chinooks and halibut. Most favour flashers but at times a dodger produces excellent results. Early on, try trailing the lure or bait 40 inches behind the flasher and then increase this distance in 2-inch intervals until the fish turn on. This tactic is usually successful right through May when the first migratory chinooks appear.

Early July should see a few chinooks to 30-plus pounds showing up in the mix, and during odd-numbered years the pink salmon fishery also starts now. By August, depending on the coho abundance, there should be good offshore fishing, but inshore anglers will still be looking for big late-run chinooks. September and October will see coho and chum fishing tapering off, with increasing interest in halibut. Then in November it's back to winter chinook fishing, starting the whole cycle over again.

## Hotspots and Fishing Tactics

"Cop Car" is one of the most popular spoon patterns.

For winter chinooks off the Victoria waterfront try the area from Saxe Point to Clover Point, around the Trial Islands, Gonzales Point, Oak Bay, "The Gap" between Discovery and Chatham islands and Ten Mile Point. At times it's not necessary to travel far in search of action because good salmon fishing is often found near the mouths of both marinas. According to Sean Moore, former manager of Pedder Bay Marina and RV Park, a good place for feeder chinooks is right in Pedder Bay around the kelp beds and just outside the mouth at the "RCN Blasting" sign. Try an anchovy or herring in a glow, glow green or glow scale Rhys Davis Anchovy Special, squirts or hoochies in white, green/white, purple haze, army truck, glo below, Irish mist or jellyfish. If you prefer spoons, try pulling a no. 4 Coyote, no. 4 Titan or no. 5 Gibbs Gator in glow white/green, glow green, green/white, black/white, army truck or cop car. Popular flasher patterns for this time of year are purple haze and plaid.

Good catches are often possible by downrigging at 100 to 115 feet anywhere from Trial Island to Albert Head, depending on the tides. Also worth investigating are the stretch between Brotchie Ledge and Finlayson Point during the flood tides and along the west side of Trial Island during the ebbs. Other productive areas, usually right on through April, are just off the Esquimalt Gravel Pit, Clover Point and Constance Bank.

When the so-called "Columbia" run starts in May, try downrigging in the stretch between Whirl Bay and Church Rock, around the Bedford Islands and Beechey Head, and southwest toward Sooke at the "Trap Shack," Secretary (Donaldson) Island, Otter Point and on up to Point No Point. An anchovy or herring in a glow, glow green or glow scale Rhys Davis Anchovy Special behind a purple haze or plaid flasher usually does the job. Increase leader lengths to, say, one at 6 feet and another up to 8 feet. If trolling squirts or hoochies, try white, green/white, purple haze, Glo Below, mint tulip or jellyfish. For spoon colours stick with those mentioned above.

Also close to Pedder Bay are Race Passage and Race Rocks; Constance Bank is just a short run northeast, and Border (Coyote) Bank is a short jog southward toward the Olympic Peninsula. A good setup is an anchovy or herring in a glow, glow green or glow scale Rhys Davis Anchovy Special behind a purple haze or plaid flasher. If trolling squirts or hoochies, try the colours mentioned above. Again, popular spoon colours include glow green, green/white, black/white, and army truck.

June usually sees good chinook fishing in all areas with early morning depths in the 40-foot range and down to 80 to 100 feet on bright, sunny days. If in doubt, a good searching setup is a 6-inch anchovy in a chartreuse or glow Rhys Davis Anchovy Special trailed 6 feet behind a purple haze flasher, trolled anywhere from 60 feet down to 160 feet. Also worth a try are purple haze and jellyfish hoochies or squirts and 4-inch Coyote, Gypsy or Titan spoons in green/glow, black/glow or army truck. Drift-jiggers might find action at the "Deep Hole" in Pedder Bay, the 120-foot hole by William Head or in close to the bluffs at Beechey Head—but watch out for swells.

Chinook fishing can be outstanding in July. On the floods and high slacks, fish the kelp beds, "The Wall" and "Deep Hole" in Pedder Bay, and the "RCN Blasting" sign. Outside of Pedder Bay, try Christopher

Point, Church Rock or the 36-metre contour line along the mouth of Whirl Bay. Also keep an eye on Alldridge Point, Beechey Head, the "Trap Shack" and the stretch between Brotchie Ledge and Trial Island. The best trolling depths are usually around 60 to 80 feet, with good setups including a purple glow, purple haze or green/silver Hot Spot flasher trailing a medium anchovy in a mint/pearl or glow Rhys Davis Anchovy Special, or jellyfish hoochies and squirts. Don't overlook those 4-inch spoons—they account for a lot of salmon.

This is also when pinks and sockeye start appearing. The odd-year abundance of pinks creates a great fishery for getting kids and casual anglers started as the often fast-paced action guarantees they will catch fish and avoid getting bored. Pinks are usually found from William Head to Otter Point, anywhere from inshore out to the first or second tide line, usually at depths between 20 and 60 feet. The most popular setup is a pink, red or orange squirt or hoochie trailing about 4 feet behind a flasher. They will also take an anchovy in a pink Rhys Davis Anchovy Special, a setup that also gives you a shot at chinooks.

The lures and tactics are similar for sockeye, which are much more difficult to catch than pinks. Those addicted to eating sockeye don't mind, though, as they claim that such good eating is worth the time and effort. Try a small green or chrome flasher trailing a pink, green or red hoochie or squirt, or a Googly-Eyed Wild Thing Sockeye Lure.

August generally sees the arrival of wild and hatchery-marked coho that provide good fishing from the Pedder Bay kelp beds right up the coast to Otter Point. Coho are usually plentiful out around the second and third tide lines, and depths seldom range much more than 60 feet. Try trolling with a hoochie, spoon, Hot Spot Apex or herring strip.

August hiding spots for big chinooks should continue to be the Pedder Bay kelp beds, in behind the Church Rock reef in Whirl Bay during flood tides and on the Bedford side during ebbs. Moving westward, on the flood try the wall between Beechey Head and Alldridge Point and on the ebbs or slack tides just inside of Beechey Head.

The original Googly-Eyed Wild Thing was developed for sockeye.

September finds northern coho on the scene, plus a few late-running chinooks, and mixed in will be the later runs of more localized sockeye, pinks, and coho. Tackle remains what you used throughout the summer, but watch for changes in productive depths as water temperatures cool. Try trolling shallow in the morning and in the evening.

## AVAILABLE MARINE CHARTS

3310 Gulf Islands—Victoria Harbour to Nanaimo Harbour
3440 Race Rocks to D'Arcy Island
3441 Haro Strait, Boundary Pass and Satellite Channel
3461 Juan de Fuca Strait, Eastern Portion
3462 Juan de Fuca Strait to Strait of Georgia
3476 Approaches to Tsehum Harbour
3641 Albert Head to Otter Point

## Marine Chart Coordinates:

| Place Names: | | Place Names: | |
|---|---|---|---|
| Alldridge Point | LAT 48°19' LONG 123°38' | Holland Point | LAT 48°25' LONG 123°22' |
| Albert Head | LAT 48°23' LONG 123°29' | Macaulay Point | LAT 48°25' LONG 123°25' |
| Becher Bay | LAT 48°20' LONG 123°37' | O'Brien Point | LAT 48°20' LONG 123°42' |
| Bedford Islands | LAT 48°19' LONG 123°36' | Oak Bay | LAT 48°26' LONG 123°18' |
| Beechey Head | LAT 48°19' LONG 123°39' | Ogden Point | LAT 48°25' LONG 123°23' |
| Bentinck Island | LAT 48°19' LONG 123°32' | Otter Point | LAT 48°21' LONG 123°49' |
| "Border (Coyote) Bank" | LAT 48°18' LONG 123°17' | Pedder Bay | LAT 48°20' LONG 123°33' |
| Brethour Island | LAT 48°41' LONG 123°19' | Point No Point | LAT 48°23' LONG 123°59' |
| Brodie Rock | LAT 48°24' LONG 123°17' | Possession Point | LAT 48°20' LONG 123°43' |
| Brotchie Ledge | LAT 48°24' LONG 123°23' | Pym Island | LAT 48°42' LONG 123°23' |
| Cattle Point | LAT 48°27' LONG 123°17' | Race Passage | LAT 48°18' LONG 123°32' |
| Charmer Point | LAT 48°41' LONG 123°21' | Race Rocks | LAT 48°18' LONG 123°32' |
| Chatham Island | LAT 48°26' LONG 123°15' | Sansum Narrows | LAT 48°48' LONG 123°34' |
| Cherry Point | LAT 48°43' LONG 123°33' | Saseenos | LAT 48°23' LONG 123°40' |
| Christopher Point | LAT 48°19' LONG 123°34' | Satellite Channel | LAT 48°43' LONG 123°26' |
| Church Island | LAT 48°19' LONG 123°35' | Saxe Point | LAT 48°25' LONG 123°25' |
| Clover Point | LAT 48°24' LONG 123°21' | Sheringham Point | LAT 48°23' LONG 123°55' |
| Constance Bank | LAT 48°21' LONG 123°21' | Sooke | LAT 48°23' LONG 123°43' |
| Discovery Island | LAT 48°25' LONG 123°14' | Sooke Basin | LAT 48°23' LONG 123°40' |
| Domville Island | LAT 48°40' LONG 123°19' | Sooke Bluffs | LAT 48°21' LONG 123°45' |
| Donaldson (Secretary) Island | LAT 48°20' LONG 123°42' | Ten Mile Point | LAT 48°27' LONG 123°16' |
| Frazer Island | LAT 48°20' LONG 123°37' | "Trap Shack" | LAT 48°19' LONG 123°41' |
| "The Gap" | LAT 48°26' LONG 123°14' | Trial Islands | LAT 48°24' LONG 123°18' |
| Gonzales Point ("Golf Links") | LAT 48°24' LONG 123°18' | Victoria Harbour | LAT 48°25' LONG 123°24' |
| Gordons Beach | LAT 48°22' LONG 123°50' | Whiffen Spit | LAT 48°21' LONG 123°45' |
| Haro Strait | LAT 48°35' LONG 123°19 | Whirl Bay | LAT 48°19' LONG 123°35' |

Between ferry traffic, the commercial fleet and an active recreational fishery, Hardy Bay is a beehive of activity during the summer months.

## Port Hardy

Thousands of anglers visit Port Hardy annually, knowing they have a better than average chance of catching trophy-sized chinooks here and—true to the town's claim of being "King Coho Country"—coho weighing up to 20-plus pounds. In addition, some of the largest halibut caught off Vancouver Island are weighed in at Port Hardy each year, along with some truly huge yellow-eye rockfish and lingcod. Anglers from around the world make annual visits to the island-studded waters of Queen Charlotte Strait where, weather permitting, day after day can be spent exploring a seemingly endless number of new areas that offer exciting, productive fishing opportunities.

**Our Information Sources**

Ian Andersen, owner, Silver Fox Charters
Corey Hayes (deceased), owner, Corey's Fishing Charters
Ken Jenkins, owner, Codfather Charters
Bill Shire, guide, Codfather Charters

**For visitor information:**

PORT HARDY VISITOR CENTRE
7250 Market Street
Box 249
Port Hardy, BC V0N 2P0
(250) 949-7622
phcc@cablerocket.com
www.ph-chamber.bc.ca

Visitors may fly to Port Hardy via Pacific Coastal Airlines scheduled flights from Vancouver. For those driving, the distances are approximately 530 km from Sidney, 500 km from Victoria, 390 km from Nanaimo and 280 km from Comox. Once north of Campbell River, the

highway meanders between high mountains blanketed with active logging areas and replanted clear-cuts in various stages of growth, from
seedlings to trees nearing maturity. It is one of the most interesting and
scenic stretches on the entire Island Highway.

Like many coastal communities, Port Hardy has suffered fluctuations and downturns in the forest industry and commercial fishery and
then in 1996 from the closure of the Island Copper Mine, which since
1971 had been a major contributor to the local economy. During the
late 1990s, however, while negative thinkers were prophesying doom
and gloom for northern Vancouver Island's largest community, it simply
didn't happen. Instead, the Quarterdeck Inn and Marina Resort went
through a major upgrading and expansion of its docks and in 1999
opened a new waterfront inn with 40 deluxe, ocean-view rooms.
Nearby, the popular Glen Lyon Inn added an entire new third floor to
their operation overlooking Hardy Bay.

Just wishful thinking by the respective owners? Hardly. Although
this community of 4,600 has 9 motels and hotels and nearly 20 bed and
breakfast operations, accommodations are hard to come by during the
summer months, which is when BC Ferries increases the number of
sailings to Prince Rupert in order to handle the tourist traffic. From
June through September the ferry arrives from Prince Rupert on alternate evenings, then departs the following morning. Ferry travellers
flood the city on arrival nights and all accommodations are booked to
capacity. In addition, from July through September the Discovery Coast
Passage ferry operates between Port Hardy, Bella Coola, Ocean Falls and
Bella Bella. It docks on alternate nights to the Prince Rupert ferry,
and thus, with passengers reserving overnight stays in Port Hardy well
in advance, finding a room on short notice ranges from difficult to
impossible.

The area has a half-dozen fishing lodges and resorts, which range
from a remote floating operation like Duval Point Lodge, accessible
only by water or floatplane, to Codfather Charters, which has accommodations located right beside the marina. There are also 5 local campgrounds so those with RVs, motor homes, campers or tents can usually
find space. Nevertheless, to avoid disappointment, booking well in
advance of the salmon fishing peak is always advised.

Forestry still plays the dominant role in the area's economy, with fish
farms and a processing plant producing another welcome boost. That
said, outdoor recreation is also important to the tourism sector.

Although eco-tourism and ocean kayaking attract an increasing number of visitors each year, recreational fishing is by far the largest contributor in terms of jobs and the generation of "out-of-town" dollars. Obviously, anglers also contribute toward the demand for accommodations.

Port Hardy offers a full range of services and amenities. The Glen Lyon Inn is noted for early morning breakfasts, I.V.'s Quarterdeck Pub for pub grub, and the Airport Inn for Chinese food. The area also boasts Hardy Buoys Smoked Fish, a large, fully modern operation where anglers can have their catch processed and prepared for shipment. It's a great place to buy live Dungeness crabs when they are available and a wide range of fresh and smoked fish. Be warned in advance that if you try their Indian Candy smoked salmon, it will become habit-forming. Those planning to use their own boats will find that the government wharf is usually plugged with commercial fishing boats throughout the summer. Moorage is available at the Quarterdeck Marina on a daily, weekly or monthly basis, but book well in advance. There is a free municipal launch ramp at the Quarterdeck Marina. It is concrete and three lanes wide, but watch the drop-off on extremely low tides. Pay parking is available at the marina office, but there is also limited free parking about two blocks from the ramp. Another free ramp is located at Bear Cove near the BC Ferry terminal. This asphalt ramp has a fairly sharp drop-off, making it an excellent place to launch small boats and car-toppers. There is ample free parking.

Hardy Bay Boat Rental offers 16½- to 19-foot boats. There are several independent fishing guides in the area, and the Port Hardy Charter Boat Association includes several experienced guides with Coast Guard-inspected cabin cruisers ranging from 20 to 40 feet.

## Weather and Water Conditions

Port Hardy enjoys a fairly moderate climate. Average winter temperatures are slightly warmer than most of Vancouver Island although it is usually a bit cooler during the summer. Rainfall ranges

Ohio resident Harry Stefanyk was fishing out of Port Hardy when he caught his first chinook salmon—a 34-pounder in the tyee class.

between 100 and 120 inches a year. Ian Andersen, skipper of the 40-foot-long *Silver Fox,* has been chartering and guiding in this area since the mid-1960s. He has been involved with several maritime rescues ranging from engine failures to capsized boats to sinkings. When he states that mariners consider the waters of Queen Charlotte Strait to be some of the most treacherous off the BC coast, believe him. Winter southeasters prevail from mid-October until May and may blow for two weeks straight without dropping below 50 km/h. Although generally considered safe, summer northwesters can also turn dangerous. Often gentle on dull, overcast days, they can build quickly to 80 km/h on clear, sunny days, creating waves to 6 feet high or more. Andersen cautions that even on nice days with calm water, it pays to watch the horizon for dark wind lines and monitor your radio for possible changes in weather conditions.

April southeasters might reduce fishing opportunities, but May through June usually offers pleasant weather. July and August can also be good but expect fog, especially in the mornings. Aside from occasional rain or windy conditions, September through mid- to late October is generally fair to good before serious winter weather sets in.

Many local anglers use 14-foot boats with 20- to 30-hp outboards, but something more substantial is recommended for fishing much beyond Hardy Bay. Offshore boats should be seaworthy and carry the minimum of a compass and VHF radio. Fog during late summer is common, so a Global Positioning System can be beneficial and radar makes moving around even safer.

## Run Timing

One of the busiest guides in the area is Ken Jenkins, who operates Codfather Charters. After visiting Port Hardy to fish for salmon and halibut in the early 1980s, he decided to move there from Edmonton, Alberta, in 1986 and go into the guiding business. He started with one boat but four years later was up to three and has been operating five for several years now. In 2006 he began replacing his aging 24-foot Bayliners with new 24-foot Sea West custom-built cabin cruisers.

According to Jenkins, feeder chinooks are available all year and the winter fishery in Hardy Bay can be quite productive. Because of rapidly changing weather conditions, popular winter areas are close to the mouth of Hardy Bay—Dillon, Daphne and Duval points and the Gordon Islands. Migratory chinooks usually start arriving toward the end of May and peak in August. However, depending on water fluctuations like the warm El Niño and chilly La Niña, runs may vary from up to three weeks early to three weeks late. As a result, migratory chinook fishing might taper off around mid-August or continue to be good until mid-September. As most fish are still early in their migrations when they arrive here, they are in prime condition. The average is 20 to 25 pounds, but 30-pounders are common and catching chinooks up to 60 pounds is quite possible. Trophies of 70 pounds have been taken on occasion.

Coho usually arrive in two waves—early and late summer. Bluebacks averaging 3 to 4 pounds start building in early July, with some of the more mature fish weighing up to 9 pounds. Early August sees coho to 12 pounds, and by month's end fish in the high teens to low 20s are often weighed in daily. Best bets for northern coho are in September but some remain in the area until well into October.

Sockeye appear as early as mid-June, peak during July and August, then dwindle by early September. They average 5 pounds but 8-pounders have been reported. Pink salmon runs are heaviest during odd years. The best fishing occurs in July and August when they average 4 to 7 pounds, though occasionally larger. While most are caught offshore, the Quatse River run attracts good numbers right into Hardy Bay. Chums generally show up in August, but with anglers still intent on chinooks and coho, most are hooked incidentally. They average 6 to 8 pounds but tackle-busters of 20-plus pounds have also been taken.

## Hotspots and Tactics

The preferred method for catching chinooks and coho is downrigging at depths of 60 to 150 feet with or without a flasher, usually with an anchovy or whole herring in a Rhys Davis Anchovy Special, herring

Maurice Hunt (left) caught this trophy-class 24-pound coho while fishing out of Port Hardy with the late Corey Hayes.

A productive and long-time favourite spoon pattern is the 50/50 brass and nickel finish.

strip in a Teaser, or a cut-plug. Dependable flasher colours are purple/gold, red/gold, jellyfish, purple haze, and green/chrome. Use a 72-inch leader for chinooks and 36 to 42 inches for coho. (Note that 40-pound-test fluoro-carbon has pretty well replaced nylon monofilament.)

Hot Spot Apex lures are popular as are pink hoochies during the early season and then, when salmon start feeding on baitfish, white, green/white, purple/pink, blue/white and army truck. If you prefer towing plugs, a selection of 4- to 7-inch Tomic Classics should include patterns no. 84, 212, 530, 602 and 632.

If schools of large pilchards or herring are present, try a Wonder Spoon or Clendon Stewart that matches their size. For herring try no. 4, 5 and 6, and for the larger pilchards a no. 6, 7 or 8. Brass/chrome is the best all-round finish, but for early mornings, dark overcast days or in dirty water use a blue pearl Clendon Stewart. For bright days and clear water switch to straight chrome. Some of the newer spoons like Coyote and Tomic also work well in similar finishes, but don't overlook green/white, black/white, blue/white and so forth.

Although anchovies are not present in the area, they work exceptionally well in a Rhys Davis Anchovy Special in purple/chrome, Betsy, glo, green/white, and chrome. Codfather Charters guide Bill Shire recommends using an anchovy 6½ feet behind a crystal lime green Gibbs flasher. If salmon are striking short, he ties a tandem setup with a no. 3/0 Gamakatsu single hook trailing about 2½ inches behind so that it is even with the bait's tail.

For pinks, sockeye and chums, the standard tactic is to troll small red, pink or pale orange hoochies in a straight line at extremely slow speeds. Jenkins recommends using a Googly-Eyed Wild Thing, which are made in Port Hardy by DJ's Lures. Sockeye are found anywhere from the surface down to about 100 feet, and putting down several lures increases your chances of multiple hookups. Good flasher colours are red/chrome, green/chrome, and Betsy. Drift-jigging is also productive. Whether the finish is painted, plated metal or holographic, matching the baitfish in size attracts chinooks and coho. For pinks, sockeye and chums, try smaller sizes in hot pink or chartreuse.

Depending on the usual variables of weather, light conditions and bait availability, several good areas for chinooks and coho are accessible to small boaters; they include the Masterman Islands at the eastern entrance to Hardy Bay and then around Dillon Point toward Peel, Round, Deer and Cattle islands, which are all located in Beaver Harbour. At the western entrance to Hardy Bay, Duval Island is fairly dependable for salmon. Continuing westward along Goletas Channel, trolling can be productive from Duval Point to Frankham Point. Weather permitting, cross Goletas to try around Duncan Island, the Gordon Islands, Heard, Bell, Hurst and Balaklava islands and westward as far as Boxer and Hussar points on Nigei Island. When pinks and sockeye are running, all of these areas can be productive.

Early in the season, before migratory salmon have moved into more

accessible areas, anglers with fast, seaworthy boats can explore farther offshore around the islands, rocks and reefs forming the Walker, Deserters and Millar groups and along the mainland shoreline from Jeannette and Browning islands and eastward to the Raynor Group.

Don Villani of Powell River was fishing out of Port Hardy when he landed this 38-pound chinook.

## AVAILABLE MARINE CHARTS

3547 Queen Charlotte Strait, Eastern Portion (Stuart Narrows, Kenneth Passage)

3548 Queen Charlotte Strait, Central Portion (Blunden Harbour, Port Hardy

3551 Jeannette Islands to Cape Caution

3574 Numas Island to Harris Island

3575 Goletas Channel to Pine Island (Bull Harbour)

3597 Pulteney Point to Egg Island

### Marine Chart Coordinates:

| Place Names: | | Place Names: | |
|---|---|---|---|
| Balaklava Island | LAT 50°51' LONG 127°37' | Gordon Islands | LAT 50°49' LONG 127°28' |
| Bear Cove | LAT 50°43' LONG 127°28' | Hardy Bay | LAT 50°44' LONG 127°28' |
| Beaver Harbour | LAT 50°42' LONG 127°24' | Heard Island | LAT 50°50' LONG 127°31' |
| Bell Island | LAT 50°50' LONG 127°32' | Hurst Island | LAT 50°50' LONG 127°35' |
| Bolivar Passage | LAT 50°54' LONG 127°33' | Hussar Point | LAT 50°51' LONG 127°39' |
| Boxer Point | LAT 50°50' LONG 127°39' | Jeannette Islands | LAT 50°55' LONG 127°25' |
| Browning Islands | LAT 50°54' LONG 127°20' | Masterman Islands | LAT 50°45' LONG 127°25' |
| Cattle Island | LAT 50°43' LONG 127°24' | Millar Group | LAT 50°55' LONG 127°26' |
| Deer Island | LAT 50°43' LONG 127°23' | Morgan Shoal | LAT 50°47' LONG 127°15' |
| Deserters Group | LAT 50°53' LONG 127°29' | Nigei Island | LAT 50°53' LONG 127°45' |
| Dillon Point | LAT 50°54' LONG 127°24' | Peel Island | LAT 50°44' LONG 127°24' |
| Duncan Island | LAT 50°49' LONG 127°33' | Raynor Group | LAT 50°53' LONG 127°14' |
| Duval Island | LAT 50°46' LONG 127°30' | Richards Channel | LAT 50°57' LONG 127°27' |
| Duval Point | LAT 50°46' LONG 127°29' | Ripple Passage | LAT 50°54' LONG 127°27' |
| Frankham Point | LAT 50°47' LONG 127°35' | Round Island | LAT 50°43' LONG 127°22' |
| Goletas Channel | LAT 50°49' LONG 127°44' | Taylor Bank | LAT 50°50' LONG 127°16' |
| Gordon Channel | LAT 50°52' LONG 127°35' | Walker Group | LAT 50°54' LONG 127°32' |

# Telegraph Cove and Blackfish Sound

Lower Queen Charlotte Sound and Blackfish Sound offer excellent salmon and bottom fishing prospects. Road access to Telegraph Cove is via a right turn off Highway 19 at a well-marked 3-way junction about 7 km southeast of Port McNeill. The first major turnoff to the left on this road leads to Alder Bay Resort, which offers 88 sites, rental accommodations, a convenience store, a laundromat, a 2-lane concrete launch ramp, a marina, moorage and other amenities. About 1 km past Alder Bay the next marked turnoff to the left leads 2.6 km to Hidden Cove Lodge, with 8 rooms in the main lodge and 3 roomy cabins. As the name implies, this operation is located in a secluded cove, and it is noted for comfortable accommodations, good service and outstanding meals.

The marina at Telegraph Cove has changed dramatically in recent years.

The paved road continues on past the Canadian Forest Products huge dryland sorting and booming grounds at Beaver Cove and ends about 12 km from the highway at Telegraph Cove, a settlement established in 1912 as the northern terminus of a telegraph line from Campbell River. Included in the popular Telegraph Cove Resort that you'll find here are a convenience store, restaurant, concrete launch ramp, 135-berth marina, boat rentals and cabins. The only fuel dock in the immediate area is located at the end of the boardwalk. Although the resort's large parking lot fills to capacity during the summer months, don't worry—there is a 120-site campground just around the corner at Bauza Cove.

**Our Information Sources**

Murray Gardham, former owner, Double Bay Resort

**For visitor information:**

Port McNeill Visitor Centre
PO Box 129
Port McNeill, BC V0N 2R0
(250) 956-3131
pmccc@island.net
www.portmcneill.net

Alder Bay and Telegraph Cove are also launching spots for several remote fishing resorts located on islands in the Blackfish Sound area. These lodges are also accessible by

The launch ramp (right) and dock at Alder Bay Resort overlooks Malcolm Island. *Charlie Cornfield photo*

The view from Port McNeill toward Blackfish Sound and the Coast Mountains.

chartered floatplanes from Vancouver, Campbell River or Port Hardy, the latter two destinations being served by daily scheduled flights from Vancouver.

## Weather and Water Conditions

Murray Gardham first fished at Double Bay when it was a floating logging camp that was periodically made available to anglers. When the owner decided to sell the operation in 1989, Gardham bought it, quit his job as a heavy-duty mechanic in Campbell River and set about the monumental task of simply keeping the camp afloat. As the years passed, he cleaned up the existing camp, built new docks, cleared and levelled some adjoining property on Hanson Island and then started constructing cabins on shore using wood that he milled right on site. He also built up a steady clientele over the years and, by the time he sold in 2002, had established an enviable reputation for running an efficient operation.

Gardham says that, while the summer months are pleasant in this area, anglers should come with warm clothing and rain gear. Blackfish Sound is fairly protected from Queen Charlotte Strait northeasters but afternoon westerlies are common. If they blow against the tide, the water can get rough. Depending on location, it is usually possible to tuck into a bay or the lee of an island until water conditions level out after the tide change. Double Bay is a good sanctuary, and you can usually find protected waters in the lee of Hanson Island and the Plumper Islands by ducking through the "Blow Hole," the winding channel located between them. If the tide is low, watch for barely submerged rocks at the channel's northern entrance and use caution during tide

What every salmon angler dreams of — a trophy chinook in the net.

changes as rapids and whirlpools often form. Once through the entrance, by sticking to the channel's centre, you should be able to avoid the kelp beds.

Blackney Passage also gets rough from Licka Point to Cracroft Point on West Cracroft Island. As this is a major thoroughfare for huge cruise ships, freighters and log carriers, whenever a large vessel approaches—especially one running with the tide—get out of its way as quickly as possible and then be prepared for the high waves resulting from its passage.

Fog is seldom a problem during spring and early summer, but from mid-August on expect it almost daily, especially during the mornings. Having suitable navigation equipment on board is a must as is knowing how to use it properly.

## Run Timing

According to Murray Gardham, immature chinooks feed in Queen Charlotte Strait, but although feeders to 15-plus pounds offer year-round sport here, they receive relatively light fishing pressure because of the area's remoteness.

During the summer months all five salmon species migrate southward through the Strait on their spawning runs, feeding voraciously along the way before funnelling through Blackfish Sound into Johnstone Strait. Fishing starts to get serious in early June, but July/August is the prime period for a mixed bag of chinooks, coho, pinks and sockeye. However, the good news doesn't end there. September finds dwindling stocks of late-running fish joined by big, tackle-punishing chum salmon and northern coho, extending the season well into October if the weather co-operates.

The first of the migratory chinooks appear about early June, followed in mid-July by pink, sockeye and coho. Thirty-pound chinooks are fairly common throughout the summer, but 50-plus pounds are real possibilities, and the record rod-and-reel-caught fish from the area weighed 75 pounds. After providing dependable action throughout the summer, migratory chinooks will have pretty well vacated Blackfish Sound by mid-September, at which time large numbers of feeder chinooks again start showing up.

A few sockeye appear as early as mid-June, but the peak is from mid-July through August, tapering off in early September. They average 4 or 5 pounds, but occasionally hit 8 or 9 pounds.

Although relatively few anglers go after chum salmon intentionally, they are gaining in popularity as word gets around about their strength and the fast action they create when hooked. Present from August until well into October, chums average 7 or 8 pounds but fish to 20 pounds or more are possible.

## Hotspots and Tactics

Weather permitting, a few local people fish for feeder chinooks over the winter months. Popular areas include Neill Ledge and the islands in Cormorant Channel, Pearse Passage and Weynton Passage. Whole, cut-plug or strip herring is the preferred bait, and downrigging the most common method of presentation. Whether or not to use flashers is a personal choice because either seems to work. If opting for a flasher, make the leader about 42 to 48 inches long. Mooching with live or cut-plug herring is also an option, but rockfish and dogfish can be a real problem at times. Green or green/white hoochies can be productive, as can Tomic plugs in pink pearl or chrome. If chinooks are feeding in shallow water, drift-jigging often produces fast-paced action, with Zzingers in pink pearl, anchovy and yellowtail the most popular lure.

Blackfish Sound is noted for yielding tyee-class chinooks like this 31½-pounder caught by Paul Gianera.

As elsewhere along the West Coast, anglers seeking migratory chinook action rely on their tide tables. These anglers are out on the water before dawn, especially if the tides are flooding before sun-up, and again during late evenings, especially when a flood happens just before dark.

Once the southward migrations start, most salmon fishing ranges from Lizard Point on the northeastern side of Malcolm Island, down past Donegal Head, the Plumper Islands and Hanson Island, through Blackney Passage to the mouth of Baronet Passage, and from Cracroft Point to the Sophia Islands at the southwestern end of West Cracroft Island. Much of the midsummer action occurs along the Plumper Islands, south to Spout Islet just past the mouth of Double Bay. Other hotspots include the mouth of Baronet Passage, from Cracroft Point across to Bell Rock and up to Parson Island. The mouth of Parson Bay can be productive, but a closure from the marker at the northern tip of Parson Island across to Red Point on Harbledown Island is in effect from mid-June to mid-October. Consult the *BC Tidal Waters Sport Fishing Guide* for the precise dates. The mouths of Whitebeach and West passages are productive at times, as is the entire southern shore of Swanson Island all the way from Freshwater Bay to Bold Head. Continuing north past Swanson is the mouth of Knight Inlet, then a cluster of islands; fish in close to these islands, heading northward right up to Wedge Island. If the water conditions are too rough on Blackfish Sound, try Weynton Passage at the mouth of Johnstone Strait, Ella Point near the mouth of Telegraph Cove, around the Wastell Islets or the Blinkhorn Peninsula.

When coho open for retention, they are often found at depths of 50 to 60 feet, so downrigging is the standard tactic. The most popular setup is a flasher and green/white hoochie. Some large coho are taken in late August, with occasional fish over 20 pounds; however, that particular run of fish stays in the area for only a week or two and then the maximum size drops back to about 12-14 pounds until well into October.

An ocean-caught chum salmon is chrome bright, far different than most caught staging off the estuaries.

The most productive sockeye tactic is trolling slowly with a small hoochie about 22 to 28 inches behind a Hot Spot, O'Ki, or Gibbs Sockeye flasher. This is also a good setup for pinks, which average 4 to 6 pounds. They are often so numerous that chinook and coho anglers consider them a nuisance, but many target them intentionally with lightweight tackle and fly-casting gear. They also enjoy some good eating as the delicate flesh of pink salmon when freshly caught is excellent and quite tasty when hot smoked. Murray Gardham uses basically the same setup for chums and suggests that, when a fish is hooked, you should slip the motor out of gear and let the other lines settle because chums will often hit a hoochie while it is sinking down slowly behind the flasher.

## AVAILABLE MARINE CHART

3546 Broughton Strait

## Marine Chart Coordinates:

| Place Names: | | Place Names: | |
| --- | --- | --- | --- |
| Alder Bay Campsite | LAT 50°34' LONG 126°55' | Licka Point | LAT 50°34' LONG 126°41 |
| Baronet Passage | LAT 50°33' LONG 126°35' | Lizard Point | LAT 50°40' LONG 126°53' |
| Bauza Cove Campground/Marina | LAT 50°33' LONG 126°49' | Malcolm Island | LAT 50°39' LONG 126°59' |
| Bell Rocks | LAT 50°33' LONG 126°39' | Mitchell Bay | LAT 50°38' LONG 126°51' |
| Blackfish Sound | LAT 50°35' LONG 126°43' | Neill Rock | LAT 50°36' LONG 127°03' |
| Blackney Passage | LAT 50°34' LONG 126°41' | Nowell Bank | LAT 50°45' LONG 126°51' |
| Blinkhorn Peninsula | LAT 50°33' LONG 126°47' | Numas Islands | LAT 50°46' LONG 126°06' |
| "Blow Hole" | LAT 50°35' LONG 126°47' | Parson Bay | LAT 50°34' LONG 126°39' |
| Bold Head | LAT 50°37' LONG 126°44' | Parson Island | LAT 50°34' LONG 126°40' |
| Broughton Island | LAT 50°49' LONG 126°45 | Pearse Islands | LAT 50°35' LONG 126°52' |
| Cormorant Channel | LAT 50°36' LONG 126°54' | Pearse Passage | LAT 50°35' LONG 126°53' |
| Cracroft Point | LAT 50°33' LONG 126°40' | Plumper Islands | LAT 50°35' LONG 126°47' |
| Donegal Head | LAT 50°38' LONG 126°49' | Port McNeill | LAT 50°35' LONG 127°06' |
| Double Bay | LAT 50°35' LONG 126°46' | Pulteney Point | LAT 50°38' LONG 127°09' |
| Egeria Shoal | LAT 50°38' LONG 126°46' | Queen Charlotte Sound | LAT 51°30' LONG 128°30' |
| Ella Point | LAT 50°33' LONG 126°49' | Red Point | LAT 50°35' LONG 126°40' |
| Foster Island | LAT 50°42' LONG 126°50' | Sophia Islands | LAT 50°32' LONG 126°38' |
| Freshwater Bay | LAT 50°36' LONG 126°42' | Spout Islet | LAT 50°35' LONG 126°45' |
| George Bank | LAT 50°44' LONG 126°58' | Stubbs Island | LAT 50°36' LONG 126°49' |
| Haddington Passage | LAT 50°36' LONG 126°00' | Swanson Island | LAT 50°37' LONG 126°42' |
| Hanson Island | LAT 50°34' LONG 126°44' | Telegraph Cove | LAT 50°28' LONG 126°17' |
| Harbledown Island | LAT 50°34' LONG 126°35' | Trinity Bay | LAT 50°39' LONG 126°55' |
| Hidden Cove | LAT 50°33' LONG 126°51' | Wastell Islets | LAT 50°33' LONG 126°49' |
| Holford Islets | LAT 50°44' LONG 126°48' | Wedge Island | LAT 50°38' LONG 126°43' |
| Johnstone Strait | LAT 50°27' LONG 126°00' | West Cracroft Island | LAT 50°33' LONG 126°23' |
| Kenneth Bay | LAT 50°50' LONG 126°00' | West Passage | LAT 50°36' LONG 126°41' |
| Knight Inlet | LAT 50°47' LONG 126°38' | Weynton Passage | LAT 50°35' LONG 126°49' |
| Ledge Rock | LAT 50°41' LONG 126°41' | Whitebeach Passage | LAT 50°35' LONG 126°40' |
| Leonard Rock | LAT 50°36' LONG 126°58' | | |

# Sayward

About 35 km northwest of Campbell River, Highway 19 slopes down into the Salmon River Valley, one of the most beautiful areas on Vancouver Island. Here, openings in the dense evergreen forest reveal grassy stretches of farmland, most with well-kept houses, barns and outbuildings. The hill eventually bottoms out where the Salmon and White rivers join, and immediately downstream from that point the road crosses a bridge that

**Our Information Sources**

Hans Schuer, fishing guide and sightseeing tour operator

**For visitor information:**

SAYWARD FUTURES SOCIETY
Box 143
Sayward, BC V0P 1R0
(250) 282-0018
sfs@saywardvalley.net
www.portofkelseybay.com

spans the single channel. About 1 km farther along is Sayward Junction, where some dramatic changes have occurred fairly recently. Charlie's Cafe, which once dominated the junction's north side, was torn down in mid-2007, leaving only a small tourist information building. However, among several new buildings on the south side are a gas station, a convenience store, a beer, wine and liquor shop and the Cyprus Tree Inn Family Restaurant and Pub. Other eateries in this area include the Cable House Café beside the river en route to Sayward, the Salmon River Inn and Restaurant in Sayward, and at least two summertime mobile operations near the marina that offer fish and chips and burgers.

A right turn at the junction leads to Sayward, a pleasant 10-km drive past more farms and private dwellings, most with neatly manicured lawns and well-tended flower gardens. While Sayward offers most modern amenities and services, they are somewhat spread out. Accommodations include Fisherboy Park, which has cabins, an RV park, and a convenience store with beer, wine and liquor; Mount H'Kusam View Lodge; Elk Haven Cottages; The Log House Retreat; Victorian Gordon Gate Manor B&B and the Mural House B&B.

Until 1979 the Island Highway ended at Kelsey Bay, located at the northwestern corner of Salmon Bay and this was the terminus for the ferry to Prince Rupert. But in the process of extending Highway 19 to Port Hardy, the highway was diverted 10 km away from Sayward to the current junction, and the ferry terminus relocated to Bear Cove in Hardy Bay. Basically, all that now remains at Kelsey Bay is the large terminus parking lot overlooking the small-craft harbour. There is a concrete, all-tide launch ramp suitable for large boats, and the launch and parking fee are reasonable. The small-craft harbour offers daily and monthly moorage, and marine fuel is available. Just beyond the small-craft harbour is the government wharf, on which is located the Sayward Futures Society office and gift shop, and "Al's Room"—a family memorial to Donald Allan Wright—which provides visitors with a public viewing room from which they can watch marine traffic and pods of orcas passing by.

To the left of the wharf is an RV park with five sites, and the Sayward Fish & Game Club launch ramp. Parking is quite limited and the narrow, curving stretch of concrete is a real challenge to those unskilled at backing up with a boat trailer. A third launch ramp, located at the end of the "MacBlo causeway," is the one most used by local anglers. To get there you must drive through the former MacBlo forestry complex, then veer right at the dryland sort and follow the well-signed road around its perimeter. The steep ramp, which once had a brutally rough, rocky driving surface, was upgraded by the Sayward Fish & Game Club in 2005. In addition, they built a narrow floating dock that makes launching and landing much easier, and there is plenty of parking. There is no charge for launching and parking but donations are appreciated.

## Weather and Water Conditions

The Salmon River Valley enjoys fairly mild, somewhat drier weather than areas to the north and south, but suitable rain gear and warm clothing are always recommended. Fog becomes a possibility from mid-August on through fall.

A map of Vancouver Island shows Johnstone Strait stretching south from Telegraph Cove for 65 km to the western tip of Hardwicke Island

Fishing in the fog is a fact of life throughout much of an Island summer, especially during the mornings.

in a 4-km-wide, fairly straight channel. At Hardwicke Point it deflects northeast up Sunderland Channel, but it also continues past the mouth of Salmon Bay before it splits around Helmcken Island into Current and Race passages. But while this Strait often appears benign, this is not small-boat water. Tidal flows in Race Passage reach 6 knots, creating tide rips that are best avoided. Southerly winds seldom cause problems but even moderate westerlies are another story, especially when blowing against a running tide. If there is a westerly wind, it usually appears during midday while mornings and evenings are often calm. Johnstone Strait is also a major thoroughfare for huge cruise ships, freighters and log carriers, and when they are running with the tide, high following waves result. While a 14-foot boat is suitable when conditions are favourable, a 16-footer or larger makes far more sense here.

The area's best-known fishing guide is Hans Schuer, a native of Hanover, Germany, who moved here in 1995 after retiring from his hair styling business in Hamilton, Ontario. After spending every available moment in his 16-foot boat learning what the area's waters had to offer, he started guiding and has since built up a satisfying number of repeat customers. He points out that if the wind comes from the northeast, you will be sheltered by Hardwicke Island. If it comes from the south, Vancouver Island offers shelter, as does West Thurlow Island from the east. "On anything but a west wind we are sheltered," he concludes, "so it's always fishable. But the west and northwest are bad—even a 5-km west wind builds up waves all the way along."

Schuer also warns that the bad riptides in the area get much worse during a west wind. He uses his tide guide to determine the difference between floods and ebbs, then avoids places that he knows are bad. He adds that one he always stays away from is at the corner of Helmcken Island.

## Run Timing

Until the 1990s the Sayward/Johnstone Strait area teemed with feeder chinooks and coho over the winter months, but such has not been the case since then. A few immature chinooks still use the area for year-round feeding, but their low numbers don't attract much interest from local anglers. Until migratory salmon start passing by, most anglers simply concentrate on halibut and other bottom fish or they fish for trout in the nearby lakes.

Although a few early chinooks start passing by in May, they are scattered and on the move so there is virtually no interest in them. The first pink salmon start showing in mid- to late July, with sockeye shortly after and then a few coho. When the stronger runs of chinooks finally appear, anglers can enjoy a truly mixed-bag fishery. Most of the pink and sockeye action has faded by the end of August, but coho and a few late-running chinooks continue to be caught. When chums enter the scene, usually in mid- to late September, they provide plenty of tackle-punishing fun throughout October and well into November.

## Hotspots and Tactics

When Hans Schuer was pointing out the best salmon areas on the Johnstone Strait marine chart to me, he simply ran his fingertip down the southern shoreline and advised fishing pretty well anywhere along it. But he was quite emphatic about always staying within 50 metres of shore because that is the route the salmon favour.

About 500 metres west of Kelsey Bay, Brasseau Bay curves into the steep shoreline and has a well-defined point on its western side. Good back eddies form on each side of this point, depending on the tidal flow. Troll in close along the kelp beds bordering the shoreline. The drop-off here is steep, so try down to 200 feet for migratory chinooks. This is also a good area for drift-jigging and lends itself to casting flies.

Downrigging is the standard operating procedure, and when it comes to lures, Schuer said he uses a small pink hoochie with a ghost stripe almost exclusively and he takes all five salmon species with it. For pinks he favours a silver flasher trimmed with red, but for chinooks, coho and sockeye he uses one trimmed with fluorescent green. For chums he prefers a white flasher and mentioned that, when stuck for one a few years earlier, he simply painted a green flasher with white house paint and it worked beautifully. He added that for chums he uses a long leader—50 to 70 inches.

Most anglers rig for pinks and sockeye with small hoochies in varying shades of pink, red or orange and trail them 16 to 28 inches behind a flasher with red, pink or green trim. At times they catch more coho that anything else with these setups, and a fair number of chinooks also hit them.

On the eastern side of Salmon Bay from Graveyard Point down to Peterson Islet be aware of the shallows that jut out from Hkusam Bay. Race Passage is productive. The steep drop-off along the southern shoreline continues, but near the eastern end of Helmcken Island it starts to shallow. Note that midway between Helmcken Island and Tyee

Point on West Thurlow Island some of the humps on Ripple Shoal are less than 10 feet from the surface.

Almost directly north of Hkusam Bay, Earl Ledge juts out from Hardwicke Island, forming an underwater ridge at the western end of Current Passage. The bottom between Hardwicke Point and Earl Ledge drops steeply to over 100 metres, but it shallows to half that depth near Earl Ledge then shallows even more in Current Passage. With tidal flows up to 9 km/h the turbulence on either side of the ledge attracts bait. The ledge's east side is quite shallow and choked with kelp, but once beyond this shelf the bottom drops away. This is a good area for drift-jigging and fly casting, but whenever downrigging you will need to monitor your depth sounder closely.

## AVAILABLE MARINE CHART

3544 Johnstone Strait (Race Passage and Current Passage)

### Marine Chart Coordinates:

| Place Names: | | Place Names: | |
|---|---|---|---|
| Althorp Point | LAT 50°28′ LONG 125°48′ | Hkusam Bay | LAT 50°23′ LONG 125°55′ |
| Artillery Islets | LAT 50°26′ LONG 125°59′ | Johnstone Strait | LAT 50°27′ LONG 126°00′ |
| Blenkinsop Bay | LAT 50°29′ LONG 126°00′ | Kelsey Bay | LAT 50°24′ LONG 125°58′ |
| Brasseau Bay | LAT 50°24′ LONG 125°58′ | Midgham Islets | LAT 50°28′ LONG 125°46′ |
| Bulkely Island | LAT 50°26′ LONG 125°44′ | Race Passage | LAT 50°23′ LONG 125°52′ |
| Chancellor Channel | LAT 50°25′ LONG 125°42′ | Ripple Shoal | LAT 50°23′ LONG 125°49′ |
| Clarence Island | LAT 50°27′ LONG 125°59′ | Salmon Bay | LAT 50°23′ LONG 125°57′ |
| Current Passage | LAT 50°25′ LONG 125°53′ | Sayward | LAT 50°23′ LONG 125°58′ |
| Earl Ledge | LAT 50°25′ LONG 125°55′ | Sunderland Channel | LAT 50°28′ LONG 125°53′ |
| Eden Point | LAT 50°24′ LONG 125°47′ | "The Shoal" | LAT 50°27′ LONG 126°02′ |
| Fanny Island | LAT 50°27′ LONG 125°59′ | Tyee Point | LAT 50°23′ LONG 125°47′ |
| Graveyard Point | LAT 50°23′ LONG 125°56′ | Wellbore Channel | LAT 50°27′ LONG 125°45′ |
| Hardwicke Island | LAT 50°26′ LONG 125°51′ | West Thurlow Island | LAT 50°25′ LONG 125°38′ |
| Hardwicke Point | LAT 50°26′ LONG 125°59′ | Yorke Island | LAT 50°27′ LONG 125°59″ |
| Helmcken Island | LAT 50°24′ LONG 125°52′ | | |

# The Great Divide

In early May the first vanguards of migratory chinooks appear in the lower Johnstone Strait, alerting Campbell River anglers that the summer salmon season is starting anew. Those anglers who head north to Ripple Point, Chatham Point and "Green Sea Bay" are first to encounter these fish, many of which are white-fleshed chinooks bound for lower Fraser River tributaries. But at Chatham Point, where Johnstone Strait splits northeast into Nodales Channel and south into Discovery Passage, the salmon schools also divide.

Most of the fish travelling via the Discovery Passage route have a fairly straight run of about 50 km to the southern end of Quadra Island, though some of them swing east into Okisollo Channel between Sonora and Quadra islands. Of these, some continue northeast through Hole in the Wall between Sonora and Maurella islands into Calm Channel, but most continue southward down Okisollo to Hoskyn Channel between Quadra and Read islands, which then joins Sutil Channel.

The fish that favour the eastern or Nodales Channel route must swim around the top end of Sonora Island to Cordero Channel where they again swing in a southerly direction. Some of these salmon branch off and head up Bute and Toba inlets on the mainland to their natal rivers, but most continue down Calm Channel to eventually rejoin the western or Discovery Passage salmon in the upper Strait of Georgia. This whole area is a confusing maze of islands large and small, providing what adds up to hundreds of kilometres of channels and passages for the fish to swim through. They are seldom in a great rush because there are usually ample stocks of baitfish on which they can feed while en route.

Because of this Great Divide in the salmon migration route, we have covered Discovery Passage and its place names first in a section we have called "Campbell River" and the eastern route in a section entitled "Heriot Bay."

# Campbell River

In the realm of saltwater fishing, Campbell River and chinook salmon are truly synonymous. While some might question whether or not the city's self-proclaimed title of "Salmon Capital of the World" is justified, it is a simple statement of fact that no other West Coast location is as well known for salmon fishing. While it can certainly be argued that a few remote northern destinations consistently produce larger fish and that some areas on Vancouver Island's west coast also yield impressive numbers of tyee-class chinooks, few of them can offer chances at all five species of Pacific salmon virtually off their respective waterfronts, and none can ever lay claim to being the official headquarters for the Tyee Club of British Columbia, the world's most exclusive fishing club. Furthermore, thanks to the confusion of islands, channels and passages located between Vancouver Island's east coast and the mainland, no other destination has so many radically different places to fish that are in such close proximity to a city. Finally, and of great importance to

Campbell River's claim of being "Salmon capital of the world" is based on its location, for it enjoys year-round salmon fishing.

anglers with limited time, Campbell River is easily accessible by air or road from the Lower Mainland.

No other community of similar size along the entire British Columbia coast is as dedicated to accommodating and servicing recreational anglers on a year-round basis. Including Quadra Island, the 45-km stretch from the Oyster River northwest to Brown Bay (known locally as Brown's Bay) offers over 30 resorts, hotels and motels, 9 campgrounds and several bed and breakfast operations. There are 10 marinas, 11 boat rental operations, a dozen or so launch ramps, and the 600-foot-long Discovery Pier right in the city, constructed specifically for fishing purposes.

There is, of course, much more than fishing to occupy the attention of visitors. Three popular golf courses handle those who are so inclined, and several operations conduct boat tours to locations where customers can view and photograph grizzly bears, black bears, orcas, porpoises, sea lions, seals, and so many bald eagles that they will probably lose count. Another popular outing for many is swimming with the salmon in the Campbell River. For a modest fee customers are provided with a wet suit, facemask, snorkel and flippers so they can join other swimmers (floaters?) on a guided tour

### Our Information Sources

Bruce Aikman, owner, Aikman's Angling
Bryon Armstrong, former owner, Painter's Lodge
Dave Fletcher (deceased), owner, Morning Sun Charters
David Manson, owner, Megan Cruising
Murray Whelan, co-owner, Tyee Marine

### For visitor information:

CAMPBELL RIVER VISITOR CENTRE
Box 400
1235 Shoppers Row
Campbell River, BC V9W 5B6
(250) 286-4636
visitorinfo@campbellriverchamber.ca
www.visitorinfo.incampbellriver.com

downstream through thousands of spawning salmon. People who enjoy
scuba diving can also keep busy. The amazingly clear ocean waters are
teeming with so much marine life that the Jacques Cousteau Society
rates the Strait of Georgia as the world's second-best coldwater diving
destination (the Red Sea is first). As a result, certified charter boat operators, guides, and instructors have made Campbell River a major dive
centre.

The area's rich aboriginal heritage is showcased in the Campbell
River Museum, which features ceremonial items, masks, carvings and
fine art. The Public Art Gallery offers tours, and the Maritime Heritage
Centre has an extensive collection of maritime artifacts, some dating
back 2,000 years. A popular "must visit" for anglers is Haig-Brown
House on the bank of the Campbell River. This restored 1923 farm-
house, known as "Above Tide," was the home of pioneer conservation-
ist and author Roderick Haig-Brown and his wife, Ann.

Visitors towing their own boats will find a good selection of launch
ramps. Starting south of town and moving northward, the Campbell
River Rotary Club public launch at Ken Forde Park has a double-wide
cement ramp that can be difficult if tides are lower than 4 feet, but there
is fairly good parking here. The Big Rock Boat Ramp—across from the
Mohawk gas station—has a good deep-water ramp, but the basin itself
is small and can be difficult to access during low tides. It also has fairly
good parking.

If you drive on through town toward Campbellton, you can access
the Discovery Harbour Marina off Spit Road. It has a two-lane-wide, all-
weather, all-tides ramp, and a floating jetty for tying up to after launching. There is ample parking. The Freshwater Marina on Baikie Drive has
a good all-tides ramp and there is ample parking. However, at low tides
you will find that following the river channel downstream or upstream
can be tricky.

## Weather and Water Conditions

April and May are reasonably mild with occasional rain squalls, June is
often unsettled and windy, and July through September is generally
pleasant. Nevertheless, always having rain gear available is a wise move.
Decent weather often continues until early October, then it's anyone's
guess. High winds and heavy rains frequently force winter chinook
anglers off the water, but there are usually more than enough good days
to keep their interest up, and on these occasions the area between

Downrigging has pretty well replaced motor-mooching as the tactic of choice for fishing off Campbell River.

Shelter and Willow points will be dotted with boats.

From the Oyster River mouth northwest to the top end of Duncan Bay, the Vancouver Island shoreline is devoid of major tide rips and fast-flowing currents. This changes dramatically at Race Point, where the marine chart cautions that strong southerly winds and flood tides can form vicious tide rips. Believe it.

Only experienced boaters with seaworthy vessels should attempt to continue northward into Seymour Narrows. Considered one of the most treacherous stretches of navigable water on the West Coast, its tidal currents can exceed 25 km/h. At its best it appears relatively benign; at its worst there are long stretches of violent, white-capped rapids and standing waves, huge whirlpools, and cave-ins (sudden drops in water level) followed by surging upheavals. While at times a frightening place to be, Seymour Narrows can provide outstanding fishing when the salmon are present and in a biting mood; however, you are advised to go there only with someone who is familiar with the area.

Whenever fishing along the western side of Quadra Island, use caution around the popular tide rips at Maud Island, Copper Cliffs, Whisky Point and the Cape Mudge lighthouse since all these areas can develop extremely rough water and occasional whirlpools. As Discovery Passage is a major travel route for large cruise ships, freighters, log carriers, tugboats and seiners, their passage often makes merely rough water downright treacherous. Give all of them a wide berth and always watch for following waves.

On the upper Strait of Georgia, venturing offshore toward Sutil Point, Mitlenatch Island or Montgomery Bank should be attempted only with reasonably fast, seaworthy boats containing the bare minimum of a working compass and a VHF radio (many now carry cell phones). This vast open area is subject to sudden southeasters and northwesters, which can quickly turn things nasty. As the weather cools, fog becomes a consideration, so having a GPS on board is recommended.

## Run Timing

Feeder chinooks from sub-legal to 25 pounds are present all year, with most of the January-February action south of Campbell River around Shelter and Willow points, though a few are taken from Discovery Pier right in town. By March, chinook numbers start to pick up from lower Discovery Passage northward to Menzies, Brown and Deepwater bays.

Some big chinook runs pass through in June and July, quite a few in the 20-pound class and some in the 30s. This tapers off around late July, which is when the sockeye and pinks show up around Chatham Point along with a few early coho vanguards.

"Tyee rowing" starts on July 15 and continues until September 15 unless decreed otherwise by the Tyee Club of BC or the Department of Fisheries and Oceans. Such closures occur on the rare occasions when there are concerns about the number of returning fish.

August is "the" month to fish the Campbell River area because, with so many migrations passing through and local fish returning to their home streams, there is so much from which to choose. This continues until September, by which time most of the local pinks have ascended their home rivers, and more local chinooks start heading up the Campbell River. The sockeye and pink migrations are pretty well over, but coho start arriving in good numbers, with chum salmon right behind them. Factor in the late-running northern coho and chums, and the saltwater fishing prospects look good through October well into

November—weather permitting, of course. And then it's time to start thinking about those feeder chinooks again.

## Hotspots and Tactics

As with elsewhere along the coast, salmon fishing around Campbell

These four tyee-class chinooks prove that fishing off of Discovery Pier can be productive.

Downrigging in lower Discovery Passage.

River fluctuates. When fish are abundant, a rank amateur might blunder into a limit catch by simply heading for the closest cluster of boats and lowering a herring or drift-jig around the outskirts. However, when salmon are scarce, producing fish takes experience and knowledge about the tides, migratory patterns, feeding habits, staging locations, tackle and techniques. Anglers lacking the time to amass this information usually hire local guides and consider the money well spent.

The best winter chinook action is around Shelter and Willow points and the Cape Mudge lighthouse, with early mornings and late evenings usually the best. The two most common tactics here are motor-mooching and downrigging. The best mooching is with live or cut-plug herring during flood tides on bright, sunny days. On dull, cloudy days switch to downrigging with a slow-rolling flasher with blue trim and either a hot pink or pink/blue hoochie on a leader ranging from 36 to 42 inches. Also productive is trolling a 5- or 6-inch no. 602 Tomic plug about 30 feet behind the cannonball, down anywhere from 50 to 150 feet.

Although bucktailing is usually associated with fall coho, feeder chinooks will take them at times during the winter months, especially if the water is relatively flat with just a slight chop. Try a large blue/white, grey/white or green/white bucktail, with or without a spinner in front, trolled quickly on or just under the surface with a ½- to 4-ounce sinker.

High-speed bucktailing will take feeder chinooks during the winter.

In early May when the first migratory chinooks appear in upper Discovery Passage, feeder chinooks in the 10- to 15-pound class can usually be found from Salmon Point on southward toward Bates Beach. Try the aforementioned Tomic plug or a green-trimmed Hot Spot flasher with a green/white hoochie on a 48-inch leader. Though many will continue fishing here for feeders, others start heading northward toward Chatham Point and "Green Sea Bay" to meet the newcomers. These early migratory chinooks are aggressive feeders that are intent on storing as much energy as possible before entering freshwater to spawn. Standard tactics include downrigging with 4-inch Tomic plugs, trolling an anchovy, herring strip, hoochie or spoon behind a flasher, and motor-mooching with a live or cut-plug herring and a 12- to 16-ounce sinker.

When pink and sockeye salmon arrive on the scene, most action is provided by small hoochies trolled behind a flasher. Sockeye are often more selective than pinks so it pays to have a good selection in varying shades of pink, red and orange. Dave Manson suggests that a good searching pattern is a small, sparse, pink hoochie behind a green flasher with a 36-inch leader. He advocates varying shades of pink because sockeye are notorious for changing their preference. He does best while downrigging at 20 to 50 feet. Occasionally he sees them deeper on the sonar—100 feet or so—but says they rarely bite until moving back closer to the surface.

Bruce Aikman points out that while sockeye like a flasher that revolves slowly, in some current conditions it might roll too fast. He added a 1-inch-wide strip of adhesive lead golf tape down one side of a flasher and discovered that the added weight staggered the blade so that it rotated slower through the water. Golf tape—available at any golf shop—has a metallic finish in a range of colours. He says that these modified flashers also work well for chum salmon later in the season.

As various salmon runs move south from upper Discovery Passage, consider following the action down through Deepwater Bay, Brown Bay, Plumper Point to North Bluff, the "Green Light" on Wilfred Point (water conditions permitting), Maud Island, Race Point, Copper Cliffs, Steep Island, April Point, Whisky Point (at Quathiaski Cove), Yaculta, and the Cape Mudge lighthouse. At times a particular hotspot might stay active for several days, while at other times it's a case of today's beehive of activity being stone dead the following day. Fortunately, one need never travel far to relocate the fish.

Although trolling with downriggers is now the most popular tactic, at one time Campbell River was considered the "motor-mooching" capital. Popular tide rips would often have 200 or more boats that averaged 14 to 20 feet long bobbing about in close proximity, with all of their occupants motor-mooching. Avoiding collisions required constant vigilance and control by the motor operator, but it usually worked quite well. Unfortunately, downrigging and motor-mooching are not compatible when conditions are crowded, so the latter have been pretty well pushed out of the picture. Nevertheless, many anglers still prefer the "hands on" approach of motor-mooching and practice it whenever possible.

The Cape Mudge lighthouse is one of the most popular spots for catching migrating chinooks as they congregate there during large ebb tides to feed on herring. As well, there are usually plenty of boats working off the south end of Quadra because needlefish are abundant at the "O-Zone" and "The Hump." A common practice is for anglers to drift with the north-flowing ebb current until they pass the lighthouse, then pull their gear and run quickly back south again to repeat the drift.

In mid-July, when the official Tyee Club rowing season starts, registrations are conducted at the clubhouse located on Tyee Spit. Registrants must abide strictly by the rules governing permissible tackle and techniques, which have remained virtually unchanged since 1924. They must use only a plug or spoon, and it's common to see a few antiques like a Wallace Highliner, Salmon Special or Lucky Louie plug,

A popular fishing area in Discovery Channel is right off the Cape Mudge lighthouse at the southern end of Quadra Island.

and even older spoons like the Gibbs-Stewart and Wonder Spoon. Fortunately, newer generation plugs and spoons also work and these are what are mostly used.

Some guides and high-liners make modifications to their lures, which might be as simple as adding a daub of paint to a spoon's surface or as involved as removing the paint from a wooden plug's tail, scraping its sides to a narrower configuration in order to speed up its tail-wagging action and then repainting it. Plastic plugs can't usually be modified, but Bruce Aikman likes his Tomic plugs to have a slower action for rowing in the Tyee Pool and finds adding a strip of lead golf tape along each side does the job. He also notes that, if a plug tends to roll over on its side, a bit of lead tape on the bottom will make it run straight.

If you plan on trying for an official Tyee pin, hiring a professional guide is strongly recommended. He or she will usually provide the tackle and lures so you know they meet all specifications. Most are intimately familiar with precisely how each pet lure works in the water and will adjust their rowing speed to create the best action possible. Although rowing is a team effort, the guide is always in charge. *Always*! The bite of a large chinook can be deceptively gentle—hardly enough to jiggle your rod tip—but the guide will be watching it like a hawk and he will tell you to "STRIKE!" Which you are expected to do instantly, not a fraction of a second later.

As various salmon runs move down both sides of Quadra Island, good action is usually found around Wilby Shoals, from Francisco Point across Sutil Channel to the bell buoy off Sutil Point on Cortes Island, Marina Reef off the south end of Marina Island, Mitlenatch Island, Sentry Shoal, Montgomery Bank and along the Vancouver Island shoreline from "Big Rock" to the Oyster River mouth.

Chums appear from mid-September until well into November, providing fair to excellent action as they move down through Discovery Passage. The two most common tactics are motor-mooching and downrigging. The general consensus is that mooching with an anchovy, cut-plug herring, or a red/purple Apex at depths of 20

One of the most popular and productive hoochie colours is "army truck."

to 100 feet is best during flood tides on bright, sunny days, but on dull, cloudy days switching to downrigging is recommended. A typical setup for trolling consists of a flasher trailing a hoochie on a leader of 36 to 42 inches. Chums can be maddeningly selective about which hoochie colour turns them on. At times it might be dark shades like black, purple/black, or army truck, and at others bright ones like pink, hot pink, pink/blue, or varying shades of red or orange. A flasher trimmed with pink or red might be the answer during one bite period and then it might be necessary to switch to blue or purple. Whichever the combination, those experienced at catching chums agree that the key is to troll slowly with a fairly slow-rolling flasher. And when you do connect, hang on as these fish are notorious for their strength and endurance.

## AVAILABLE MARINE CHARTS

3513 Strait of Georgia, Northern Portion
3538 Desolation Sound
3540 Approaches to Campbell River
3539 Discovery Passage and Seymour Narrows

## Marine Chart Coordinates:

| Place Names: | | Place Names: | |
|---|---|---|---|
| April Point | LAT 50°04' LONG 125°14' | North Bluff | LAT 50°08' LONG 125°21' |
| "Big Rock" | LAT 50°59' LONG 125°13' | Okisollo Channel | LAT 50°17' LONG 125°12' |
| Brown Bay | LAT 50°10' LONG 125°22' | Oyster River | LAT 49°52' LONG 125°07' |
| Campbell River | LAT 50°02' LONG 125°16' | "O-Zone" | LAT 49°59' LONG 125°10' |
| Campbell River C | LAT 50°01' LONG 125°14' | Plumper Point | LAT 50°10' LONG 125°21' |
| Cape Mudge | LAT 50°00' LONG 125°11' | Quadra Island | LAT 50°12' LONG 125°15' |
| Copper Cliffs | LAT 50°06' LONG 125°16' | Quathiaski Cove | LAT 50°03' LONG 125°13' |
| Deepwater Bay | LAT 50°11' LONG 125°20' | Salmon Point | LAT 49°53' LONG 125°07' |
| Discovery Passage | LAT 50°08' LONG 125°21' | Sentry Shoal | LAT 49°54' LONG 124°59' |
| Discovery Pier | LAT 50°02' LONG 125°14' | Seymour Narrows | LAT 50°09' LONG 125°21' |
| Duncan Bay | LAT 50°05' LONG 125°18' | Shelter Point | LAT 49°56' LONG 125°11' |
| Francisco Point | LAT 50°01' LONG 125°09' | Steep Island | LAT 50°05' LONG 125°15' |
| Frenchman's Pool | LAT 50°03' LONG 125°15' | Tyee Pool | LAT 50°03' LONG 125°15' |
| Gowlland Harbour | LAT 50°04' LONG 125°13' | Tyee Spit | LAT 50°03' LONG 125°15' |
| Gowlland Island | LAT 50°04' LONG 125°14' | Whisky Point | LAT 50°03' LONG 125°13' |
| "Hump, The" | LAT 49°59' LONG 125°09' | Wilby Shoals | LAT 50°59' LONG 125°08' |
| Kuhushan Point (Salmon Point) | LAT 49°53' LONG 125°07' | Wilfred Point ("Green Light") | LAT 50°08' LONG 125°21' |
| Maud Island | LAT 50°37' LONG 125°36' | Willow Point | LAT 49°58' LONG 125°12' |
| Menzies Bay | LAT 50°07' LONG 125°23' | Yaculta | LAT 50°01' LONG 125°12' |
| Mitlenatch Island | LAT 49°57' LONG 125°00' | Yellow Island | LAT 50°08' LONG 125°19' |
| Montgomery Bank | LAT 49°54' LONG 124°55' | | |

The Quadra Island–Cortes Island ferry crosses Sutil Channel frequently each day.

## Our Information Sources

Dave Fletcher (deceased), owner,
Morning Sun Charters
Ed Jordan, owner, Sutil Charters
David Manson, owner, Megan
Cruising
Murray Whelan, co-owner, Tyee
Marine

## For visitor information:

CAMPBELL RIVER VISITOR CENTRE
Box 400
1235 Shoppers Row
Campbell River, BC V9W 5B6
(250) 286-4636
visitorinfo@campbellriverchamber.ca
www.visitorinfo.incampbellriver.com

# Heriot Bay

Campbell River is in an excellent starting point for anglers to run northwest through upper Discovery Passage and Seymour Narrows and right up into Johnstone Strait where the southward salmon migrations can be intercepted. However, an even closer departure point for Johnstone Strait—one that dispenses with having to run through Seymour Narrows twice in one day—is Heriot Bay on the east coast of Quadra Island. From a saltwater angler's point of view this small, quiet community is possibly one of the best-kept secrets on Quadra Island. At times salmon are available virtually right off its waterfront, and anyone seeking bottom fish needn't travel far. A quick run to the south end of Quadra Island puts anglers onto popular areas like Francisco Point, Wilby Shoals and the Cape Mudge lighthouse, and within reasonable running distances northward are Stuart Island and Toba and Bute inlets.

Heriot Bay is reached by taking the ferry from Campbell River to Quathiaski Cove on Quadra Island, a 3-km journey lasting about 10 minutes. Once ashore, an 8-km drive northwest along West Road leads to the Cortes Island ferry ramp, and just beyond the ramp are the Heriot Bay Inn and the government wharf.

Virtually all of the services and amenities required for planning everything from day trips to season-long fishing vacations are available at Heriot Bay. At the corner of West and Heriot Bay roads is the Quadra Island Market, a small shopping mall that offers a full range of groceries, baked goods, fresh meats and produce, liquor, fishing tackle and ice as well as local arts and crafts and post office services.

If you head southeast along Taku Road toward Rebecca Spit, you will find Taku Resort on the western shore of Drew Harbour. Shaded by a grove of tall evergreens, this resort offers fully equipped apartments and A-frame cabins in a well-kept setting, a fully serviced trailer park, a launch ramp, and about 500 feet of dock space. And if you don't feel like cooking, there is a family restaurant just a short walk away. Outside the entrance to Rebecca Spit Provincial Park is the We-Wai-Kai Campsite, owned and operated by the Cape Mudge Indian Band. It offers 140 sites, a convenience store, showers, laundromat and sani-dump.

The narrow finger of Rebecca Spit forms a natural, 2-km-long breakwater that protects Heriot Bay and Drew Harbour from southeasterlies blowing off the upper Strait of Georgia. There is a good concrete launch ramp on the gently sloping beach along the inshore side and two nearby parking areas. The road ends at a parking lot midway along the spit and a trail leads from there to the northern end. From this vantage point can be seen local fishing areas: north toward the Breton Islands at the mouth of Hoskyn Channel, northeasterly across Sutil Channel toward the westernmost tip of Cortes Island, and east toward Marina Island and Marina Reef. To the west of the Spit, nestled between the Cortes Island ferry slip and the government wharf, is the landmark Heriot Bay Inn, built in 1894. In addition to hotel rooms, pub, restaurant and tackle shop, it offers ocean-view cottages, fully serviced waterfront RV sites, a private marina with available docking space, boat rentals and refuelling services. The nearby government wharf has a good concrete launch ramp and a fair-sized parking lot. As with most small coastal communities, docking space is at a premium.

A channel marker on the western side of Quadra Island.

## Weather and Water Conditions

Ed Jordan grew up on Quadra Island and has lived at Heriot Bay since the 1960s. He started fishing the local waters in the mid-1970s and has operated Sutil Charters and a water taxi service there since 1987, so his knowledge and experience about the area and its fishing locations make him an excellent source of information. According to Ed, April and May are reasonably mild with occasional rain squalls, June can be unsettled and windy, and July through September is generally good. Decent weather often continues until early October, after which it's anyone's guess. The prevailing winds are southeasters that blow in unhindered from the Strait of Georgia. Westerlies are fairly well dampened by the sheer bulk of Quadra and Read islands.

The Quadra Island shoreline between the mouth of Hoskyn Channel and Francisco Point is devoid of the tide rips and fast-flowing currents so common on the opposite side of the island. A 14-foot boat with a 20-hp outboard is a reasonable choice for fishing local waters, although fast, seaworthy boats like Ed's 22-foot Bayliner are recommended for longer runs. As fall weather cools, fog becomes a reality, so in addition to equipping your boat with a dependable compass and a depth sounder, we recommend a Global Positioning System.

## Run Timing

Some feeder chinooks are present all year, but most of the dependable January-February action for them is south of Campbell River around Shelter and Willow points.

After the first migratory chinooks appear at the lower end of Johnstone Strait in early May, those taking the northeasterly route from Chatham Point through Nodales Channel swing in a southerly direction again at Cordero Channel, which takes them between Sonora Island and Stuart Island. At Stuart Island, fish destined for rivers flowing into Bute Inlet will swing north, while the remainder continue on down Calm Channel toward Sutil Channel on the west side of Cortes Island or Lewis Channel on its eastern side. However, some may swing westward through the Hole in the Wall between Sonora and Maurelle islands, which leads them into Okisollo Channel, while others may swim past Maurelle Island and turn west at Whiterock Passage between it and Read Island, which also leads to Okisollo. This passage continues down to Surge Narrows and Hoskyn Channel, which joins Sutil Channel at the bottom end of Read Island.

In the meantime, back in Calm Channel, some fish have swung north at Raza Island either through Raza Passage or Deer Passage then southward again through Pryce Channel toward Toba Inlet and Homfray Channel. Fish heading for streams in Toba will again bear north while the remainder continue southwest down Homfray Channel between East Redonda Island and the mainland. . . that is, except for those that turn into Waddington Channel between West and East Redonda islands, which eventually leads back into Homfray Channel and Desolation Sound. And believe it or not, after travelling southward through all of this confusion of channels and passages, most of the eastern route chinooks will eventually gather together in the upper Strait of Georgia with those that took the Discovery Passage western route. At that point they will all go on a major feeding binge before continuing their respective journeys.

As pinks and sockeye arrive on the scene in late July, anglers again travel northward to meet them, and they repeat this in September when the coho runs increase, followed quickly by the chums. Some of the latter two species are usually available until well into November.

## Hotspots and Tactics

Popular early season spots are Johnstone Strait, "Green Sea Bay," Chatham Point and upper Discovery Passage. Hall Point and Denham Islet are excellent at times as are the Ramsay Arm area, Frances Bay and Raza Island. While fishing for feeder chinooks, you can usually find uncrowded areas behind Cortes Island, Redonda Island and in Teakerne Arm. In April and May some migratory fish start showing up.

Popular early season setups are a cut-plug herring; a Hot Spot green Stryper flasher and glow/green hoochie with a leader from 48 to 72 inches long; or 5- to 6-inch-long no. 186, 191 and 349 Tomic plugs. Try trolling or downrigging these at depths of 30 to 130 feet. Large bucktails, hoochies or Apex lures trolled on or near the surface with a ½- to 4-ounce sinker are also productive at times.

The lower end of Read Island usually yields feeder chinooks during the springtime and right into June. Good toward the end of May for

191 Tomic Plug

Radiant Mini Plankton

migratory fish are Viner Point, "Frederic Bay" (at the mouth of Evans Bay) and right on up to Whale Passage between Cortes and Read islands. About midway along the western shore of Marina Island the beach narrows where it encounters a steep drop-off. This can be productive if you troll in close to shore.

When sockeye are present, try a red-trimmed silver flasher and a hot pink hoochie with a glow stripe on a 24-inch leader. If they are present but not biting, start adjusting the leader length in 2-inch intervals. At times 20 inches will turn them on, at others 26 or even 28 inches. The same basic setup works well for pinks, but they can be equally fussy about leader lengths and even more so about the colour. Most guides carry every shade of pink hoochie available plus those that combine pink with white, blue, green and glow.

## AVAILABLE MARINE CHARTS

3513 Strait of Georgia, Northern Portion
3538 Desolation Sound
3540 Approaches to Campbell River

## Marine Chart Coordinates:

| Place Names: | | Place Names: | |
|---|---|---|---|
| Bute Inlet | LAT 50°21' LONG 125°06' | Mitlenatch Island | LAT 49°57' LONG 125°00' |
| Calm Channel | LAT 50°19' LONG 125°05' | Nodales Channel | LAT 50°24' LONG 125°20' |
| Campbell River C | LAT 50°01' LONG 125°14' | Okisollo Channel | LAT 50°17' LONG 125°12' |
| Chatham Point | LAT 50°20' LONG 125°26' | Pryce Channel | LAT 50°18' LONG 124°50' |
| Cordero Channel | LAT 50°26' LONG 125°33' | Quadra Island | LAT 50°12' LONG 125°15' |
| Cortes Island | LAT 50°07' LONG 125°59' | Quathiaski Cove | LAT 50°03' LONG 125°13' |
| Deer Passage | LAT 50°20' LONG 125°26' | Ramsay Arm | LAT 50°23' LONG 125°58' |
| Denham Islet | LAT 50°17' LONG 124°58' | Raza Island | LAT 50°18' LONG 125°00' |
| Desolation Sound | LAT 50°07' LONG 124°47' | Raza Passage | LAT 50°20' LONG 125°00' |
| Discovery Passage | LAT 50°08' LONG 125°21' | Read Island | LAT 50°14' LONG 125°05' |
| "Dogfish Bay" | LAT 50°02' LONG 125°09' | Rebecca Spit | LAT 50°06' LONG 125°11' |
| Drew Harbour | LAT 50°06' LONG 125°11' | Sentry Shoal | LAT 49°54' LONG 124°59' |
| East Redonda Island | LAT 50°14' LONG 124°43' | Sonora Island | LAT 50°22' LONG 125°15' |
| Frances Bay | LAT 50°20' LONG 125°02' | Stuart Island | LAT 50°23' LONG 125°08' |
| Francisco Point | LAT 50°01' LONG 125°09' | Surge Narrows | LAT 50°14' LONG 125°09' |
| "Frederic Bay" | LAT 50°11' LONG 125°04' | Sutil Channel | LAT 50°08' LONG 125°04' |
| Frederick Arm | LAT 50°29' LONG 125°16' | Sutil Point | LAT 50°01' LONG 124°59' |
| Green Sea Bay | LAT 50°20' LONG 125°24' | Teakerne Arm | LAT 50°11' LONG 124°52' |
| Hall Point | LAT 50°27' LONG 125°17' | Thurston Bay | LAT 50°22' LONG 125°19' |
| Heriot Bay | LAT 50°06' LONG 125°13' | Toba Inlet | LAT 50°25' LONG 124°35' |
| Hole in the Wall | LAT 50°19' LONG 125°10' | Twin Islands | LAT 50°02' LONG 124°56' |
| Homfray Channel | LAT 50°15' LONG 124°38' | Viner Point | LAT 50°08' LONG 125°08' |
| Hoskyn Channel | LAT 50°11' LONG 125°08' | Waddington Channel | LAT 50°13' LONG 124°43' |
| Johnstone Strait | LAT 50°27' LONG 126°00' | West Redonda Island | LAT 50°12' LONG 124°53' |
| Lewis Channel | LAT 50°11' LONG 124°56' | Whale Passage | LAT 50°12' LONG 125°02' |
| Marina Island | LAT 50°04' LONG 125°03' | Whiterock Passage | LAT 50°15' LONG 125°06' |
| Marina Reef | LAT 50°02' LONG 125°03' | Wilby Shoals | LAT 50°59' LONG 125°08' |
| Maurelle Island | LAT 50°17' LONG 125°09' | | |

The waters off the Comox Valley are devoid of tide rips and whirlpools.

### Our Information Sources

Dan Boudreau, owner, Gone Fishin', Courtenay
Doug Field, owner, Buzz Bomb/Zzinger Lures, Courtenay
Vern Friesen, owner, Denverlene Charters, Comox
Brian Taylor, co-owner, King Coho Resort, Comox
Gordon Webb, former owner, Deep Bay Fishing Resort, Deep Bay

### For visitor information:

COMOX VALLEY VISITOR CENTRE
2040 Cliffe Avenue
Courtenay, BC V9N 2L3
(250) 334-3234
visitorinfo@comoxvalleychamber.com
www.comoxvalleychamber.com

# Comox Valley

The Comox Valley sprawls over a vast, fairly flat expanse of dense second-growth evergreen forest interspersed with cedar swamps, open farm lands, one large lake and several smaller ones, and waterways that range from dozens of tiny creeks to 8 rivers. To the north the Valley shares the Oyster River with neighbouring Campbell River; the Courtenay River system consists of the Tsolum and Puntledge rivers. The Cruickshank River flows into Comox Lake, which drains into the Puntledge, which in turn is joined by the Browns River. South of Courtenay are the Trent River, which passes through Royston, and the Tsable River, which enters the ocean at the top end of Fanny Bay.

The Valley sweeps down from the steep, rugged Beaufort Mountains to the eastern shoreline of Vancouver Island, where the upper Strait of Georgia's tortuous shoreline overlooks the Inside Passage and the jagged peaks of the Coast Mountains on the mainland. It encompasses the city of Courtenay, the town of Comox, the village of Cumberland, and the seaside communities of Fanny Bay, Buckley Bay, Union Bay, Royston and Saratoga Beach. There are also fair-sized unincorporated communities established on Denman and Hornby islands as well as on

Mount Washington. The combined population at time of writing (2008) was hovering around the 65,000 mark.

The Comox Valley's claim to being "The Outdoor Recreation Capital of Canada" might sound like hyperbole generated by the local Chamber of Commerce, but the impressive range of year-round outdoor activities available are unmatched elsewhere on Vancouver Island. The Beaufort Mountains overlooking the Valley have some of the deepest snow conditions found in North America, which accounts for the world-class downhill and cross-country skiing that can be accessed from Mount Washington Alpine Resort. Adjoining it is Strathcona Park, which is criss-crossed with hiking trails, many leading to alpine lakes that provide excellent rainbow trout fishing; horse rentals are available here for guided trail rides. Lower elevation lakes yield good catches of cutthroat and rainbow trout and some also have Dolly Varden. Most rivers have seasonal runs of summer- and/or winter-run steelhead, sea-run cutthroat trout, plus coho, pink and chum salmon. In addition, the Puntledge River has both summer- and fall-run chinooks and is also popular with rockhounds, fossil hunters, canoeists, and kayakers. Hunters have a good variety of big game at hand plus upland game birds and several species of waterfowl.

Much to the delight of birders and nature photographers, in addition to large resident populations of songbirds, raptors, ducks, geese and other waterfowl, the Comox Valley is visited each year by over-wintering trumpeter swans. Each February the Trumpeter Swan Festival celebrates the annual arrival of about 2,000 of these large, graceful birds. For those so inclined there are 7 golf courses and 13 public tennis courts, as well as rental facilities for wind surfing, sailing, ocean kayaking, and even sky diving. Well-travelled scuba divers claim that the waters off Denman and Hornby islands contain some of the most spectacular underwater scenery found anywhere in North America.

However, when all is said and done, if the number of small boats observed at the popular salmon haunts that border the Comox Valley is any indication, there is a good possibility that during the summer months saltwater fishing attracts more people than all of the other outdoor activities combined. That these anglers enjoy good success is no accident for the area is centred between Campbell River and Qualicum Beach, both of which have efficient salmon hatcheries that produce chinook, coho, pink and chum salmon, and several million more juvenile salmon are added to the system each year by two hatcheries on the

Puntledge River. The Comox Valley shoreline closely borders a migration route for wild and hatchery-reared salmon from the Lower Mainland, Washington and Oregon. In addition, many chinooks actually rear in this area, feeding all year round on the abundant stocks of shrimp, squid, herring and needlefish.

Visitors trailering their own boats will find a range of commercial and public launch ramps throughout the area: Miracle Beach, Kitty Coleman Beach,

The lighthouse on Chrome Island is off the southern end of Denman Island.

Jasper's Resort, Bates Beach Resort, Point Holmes, Comox Marina, Royston, Union Bay, Fanny Bay and Deep Bay as well as on Hornby Island. Some resorts have boat rentals, and there are several experienced, well-equipped fishing guides available.

## Weather and Water Conditions

The Comox Valley enjoys a moderate climate, which is further enhanced by the rain shadow effect provided by the Beaufort Mountains. It is common to see a line of dark rain clouds ending directly over the mountains, indicating that the Island's west coast is getting heavy rain while the east coast basks under relatively cloud-free skies.

April and May are fairly summer-like, but June produces unsettled weather and windy conditions. July through September is usually decent and even early October can be surprisingly pleasant at times. After that, expect typical unsettled West Coast weather until spring.

This is ideal water for small boats as there are no major tide rips or fast-flowing currents, but you must always monitor the wind conditions. Southeasters and northwesters can form quickly, creating problems for boaters trying to haul out along an exposed shoreline. The Comox–Powell River ferry slip provides a good haven for waiting out a storm, and small boats can be beached on the sloping, sandy shoreline if need be. Another option is to head for Comox Harbour, which is protected by Goose Spit, or get into the lee of Hornby or Denman islands.

Venturing to offshore reefs and banks should be attempted only with reasonably fast, seaworthy boats, preferably with a GPS to get you home should fog set in, which can happen starting around early September.

Pink salmon are extremely popular with anglers who target them from various beaches by casting flies or small lures.

## Run Timing

Feeder chinooks are present all year, but their numbers are bolstered about mid- to late May with the appearance of migratory fish weighing up to 30-plus pounds. Brian Taylor uses the Victoria Day weekend— plus or minus a couple of days—as a guideline for the arrival of migratory chinooks. Some are heading for the Fraser and Columbia systems, but a summer run of chinooks homes in on the Puntledge River.

Pink salmon, most abundant during odd years, show up around late July and create a popular beach fishery. However, when sockeye pass by on their southward migration, they stay out in the centre of the Strait of Georgia, generally favouring the mainland side for this is where their home streams are located. As a result, there is seldom any concentrated effort on sockeye but they are often caught incidentally while fishing offshore for pinks.

In August and September fall-run chinooks that are returning to the Puntledge River appear in local waters, while those returning to the Qualicum and Little Qualicum rivers will be feeding around the southern ends of Denman and Hornby islands. When chum salmon arrive in September, relatively few anglers fish for them intentionally in the ocean, but there is a popular retention fishery for them in the Puntledge River from October 1 to November 30.

# Hotspots and Tactics

NOTE: If fishing out of Comox, always consult the *BC Tidal Waters Sport Fishing Guide* beforehand to determine the Comox Harbour closure period and where the boundaries are located.

Feeder chinooks are present all year, with the most heavily fished stretches located between Miracle Beach and Seal Bay, in Lambert Channel and around the southern ends of Denman and Hornby islands. A spot to keep in mind is the 60-metre trench between the ferry terminals on Denman and Hornby islands. This is a relatively small area but at times it attracts and holds a fair number of salmon in the 10- to 15-pound range. A productive setup is a 4-inch Prism Coyote or 576h Tomic Honeycomb spoon trolled close to the bottom. Try one behind a flasher on a 6- or 7-foot leader and one without a flasher. If the action slows during slack tide, head for Tribune Bay and fish close to the sandy bottom well out along the 60- to 75-metre contour lines.

Comox Harbour usually has an abundance of feeders from December through February; however, it also has an excessively large population of harbour seals that makes landing a hooked salmon virtually impossible. If you can stand the frustration, try drift-jigging, mooching a live herring or slow-trolling with a nickel or nickel/brass Tom Mack behind a 1- to 4-ounce sinker.

Feeder chinook fishing really heats up from Bates Beach to the southern ends of Hornby and Denman islands during the annual herring spawn, which usually occurs some time in March. Downrigging is preferred as much of the action is found at depths of 100 to 200 feet. The preferred bait is an anchovy or herring but don't overlook spoons or plugs.

Once migratory chinooks are in the mix, Brian Taylor recommends trying a 7-inch no. 602 Tomic Plug about 25 to 30 feet behind the cannonball and trolled a bit faster than normal at depths of 50 to 150 feet. During July and August when dogfish might prove a nuisance for those using bait, he suggests switching to a 7-inch no. 118 Tomic plug, which incorporates a touch of green in the back.

Offshore, Montgomery Bank is popular for both salmon and bottom fish. Concentrate on its southern slopes but keep a weather eye out for wind. A run across to the waters between Grant Reefs and the eastern shore of Harwood Island can be productive if bait is present, as can the area between Vivian Island and Favada Point. A popular stretch for trolling is along the northeastern shore of Denman Island from Komass

Bluff and Palliser Rock over to Cape Lazo. Between Vancouver Island and Denman Island, Baynes Sound is spotty at best, but if herring happen to move in, the salmon will follow and it can be surprisingly productive. A good area to monitor is between Denman and Ships points.

Once the coho season opens, try for them around Lambert Channel and along the kelp beds near Cape Gurney on Hornby Island. Good numbers of chinooks are often found along the drop-offs near Phipps Point. At the southern ends of Hornby and Denman islands the presence of resident herring makes the stretch between Chrome Island and Flora Islet a prime year-round area for feeder chinooks and then migratory chinooks and coho later on. The area around Norris Rocks can be quite productive, but as harbour seals get most of the hooked salmon, anglers tend to avoid it.

Depending on timing and weather conditions, hoochies and Hot Spot Apex lures in varying shades of pinks and reds are popular early season lures. This changes about mid-May when larger salmon start feeding on baitfish, and then herring strip in a Rhys Davis teaser becomes popular, its length and width depending on whether herring or needlefish are most abundant. If more action is desired, the strip may be trailed behind a dodger or flasher. Drift-jigging is one of the most popular fishing techniques in the area, with the hands-down favourites being Buzz Bombs, Zzingers, Spinnows and Zeldas, all of which are manufactured in Courtenay.

Three popular pink salmon beach patterns.

Pike's P.D.

Siminiuk's Pink Tide

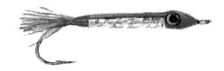

Limber's Pink Candy

During peaks of pink salmon abundance, many anglers do well by casting flies and lures from shallow beaches between King Coho Resort and the ferry slip, between Point Holmes and Goose Spit and along the Comox waterfront. Again, be aware that seals can be a real problem.

From April through September, numerous anglers cast from along the beach near King Coho Resort. At times this popular fishery is surprisingly productive as the steeply sloping beach borders a major feeding area. Long casts are seldom required because the bottom drops away so sharply, and salmon—mostly chinooks—are often within 200 feet of the beach. Coho usually remain farther offshore, but in late September and early October northern coho and chums move within easy casting range.

Surf casting attracts everyone from kids to seniors, and the equipment used ranges from trout-weight spinning outfits to long rods and free-spool casting reels with ample line capacity. Casting from the beach requires patience and vigilance because, unlike fishing from a boat, anglers must wait for the salmon to come to them. Those lacking experience usually hit the beach and cast blindly until they either hook a salmon—which happens occasionally—or they grow weary, which is more often the case. Old hands simply find a log or soft rock to sit on and then watch the water for signs of activity. Should a salmon swirl or baitfish suddenly start skittering across the surface, they walk quickly to the water's edge and lob out their lures. If a fish fails to cooperate, they give it a few minutes at most, then return to their seats. Although a few chinooks of 30-plus pounds are landed here each season, many are lost because the seals get them or the anglers simply can't hang onto them. As one regular commented, "Having 200 yards of line on your reel doesn't do any good if the fish runs 300 yards."

The largest authenticated chinook caught from the beach was a 51.1-pounder landed by Comox resident Winston Murphy on August 3, 1987. A week later, Sam Horton of North Vancouver beached a 49-pounder. Murphy's fish fell to a pink pearl Zzinger, Horton's to a pink pearl Buzz Bomb. For some strange reason pink pearl has remained the favourite lure colour among surf casters ever since.

Gil Dicesare of G&M Fishing Charters caught this brace of chinooks off the southern end of Hornby Island with a Coyote Prism spoon trailed behind a Hot Spot flasher.

## AVAILABLE MARINE CHARTS

3513 Strait of Georgia, Northern Portion
3527 Baynes Sound (Comox Harbour)

### Marine Chart Coordinates:

| Place Names: | | Place Names: | |
|---|---|---|---|
| Ajax Bank | LAT 49°39' LONG 124°43' | Harwood Island | LAT 49°52' LONG 124°39' |
| Bates Beach | LAT 49°46' LONG 124°58' | Hornby Island | LAT 49°32' LONG 124°40' |
| Baynes Sound | LAT 49°29' LONG 124°45' | Jasper's Resort | LAT 49°46' LONG 124°58' |
| Buckley Bay | LAT 49°31' LONG 124°51' | King Coho Resort | LAT 49°44' LONG 124°54' |
| Cape Gurney | LAT 49°31' LONG 124°36' | Kitty Coleman Beach | LAT 49°47' LONG 124°59' |
| Cape Lazo | LAT 49°42' LONG 124°52' | Komass Bluff | LAT 49°35' LONG 124°47' |
| Chrome Island | LAT 49°28' LONG 124°41' | Lambert Channel | LAT 49°30' LONG 124°42' |
| Comox Harbour | LAT 49°40' LONG 124°57' | Miracle Beach Provincial Park | LAT 49°51' LONG 125°06' |
| Comox-Powell River ferry slip | LAT 49°45' LONG 124°55' | Montgomery Bank | LAT 49°54' LONG 124°55' |
| Courtenay | LAT 49°41' LONG 124°59' | Norris Rocks | LAT 49°29' LONG 124°39' |
| Cumberland | LAT 49°37' LONG 124°02' | Palliser Rock | LAT 49°37' LONG 124°50' |
| Deep Bay | LAT 49°28' LONG 124°44' | Phipps Point | LAT 49°42' LONG 124°43' |
| Denman Island | LAT 49°33' LONG 124°48' | Royston | LAT 49°39' LONG 124°57' |
| Denman Point | LAT 49°33' LONG 124°51' | Saratoga Beach | LAT 49°51' LONG 124°06' |
| Exeter Shoal | LAT 49°39' LONG 124°39' | Seal Bay | LAT 49°46' LONG 123°58' |
| Fanny Bay | LAT 49°30' LONG 124°49' | Ship Point | LAT 49°30' LONG 124°48' |
| Favada Point | LAT 49°44' LONG 124°38' | Tribune Bay | LAT 49°31' LONG 124°37' |
| Flora Islet | LAT 49°31' LONG 124°34' | Union Bay | LAT 49°35' LONG 124°53' |
| Goose Spit | LAT 49°40' LONG 124°55' | Vivian Island | LAT 49°50' LONG 124°42' |
| Grant Reefs | LAT 49°53' LONG 124°48' | | |

# Parksville–Qualicum Beach

Parksville and Qualicum Beach are popular vacation destinations noted for their 6 golf courses and wide, gently sloping sandy beaches that are ideal for swimming. They also border areas that attract saltwater anglers, most of whom set forth from the French Creek Marina, located midway between these communities. One of the busiest marinas on Vancouver Island's east coast, it is centrally located between three well-known fishing areas: the Little Qualicum River 10 km to the northwest, Lasqueti Island 12 km to the north and Ballenas Channel 15 km to the southeast. With this range of fishing prospects within reasonable running time, anglers have an excellent degree of flexibility during those periods when the salmon are moving around and must be actively hunted.

The marina has excellent, deep-water, twin concrete ramps that permit launching and hauling out large boats even during low tides. Because the ramps are steep, however, hauling out at low tide with a

Anglers fishing between Parksville and Qualicum Beach usually put in at the French Creek Marina.

### Our Information Sources

Dick Brune, former owner, French Creek Store and Charters
Glen Massick, owner, AGM Outdoorsman's Pit Stop, Parksville

### For visitor information:

PARKSVILLE VISITOR CENTRE
Box 99
Parksville, BC V9P 2G3
(250) 248-3613
www.chamber.parksville.bc.ca

heavy boat might prove problematic because of the algae on the driving surface. Fortunately, simply waiting for the tide to come in usually solves the problem. There is ample parking available for vehicles and trailers. The marina complex offers several amenities and services, including a popular pub that is noted for its wide range of traditional and hearty pub grub and an upstairs restaurant that caters to those who prefer fine dining in bright, pleasant surroundings. Like most marinas along the eastern coast of Vancouver Island, this well-kept operation often becomes plugged to overflowing. As many commercial fishermen live in the area, once the commercial season ends the harbour is often congested right to its mouth. Good moorage spots in local waters are at a premium, so if planning to combine cruising with fishing, consider checking out Lasqueti Island where Scottie Bay, Orchard Bay and False Bay offer excellent moorage.

French Creek House Resort consists of a campground, cottages with one to three bedrooms, a sports complex that includes a fitness room, indoor swimming pool, sauna, showers, laundry facility, and grocery store. Fishing and sailing charters are available at the office. The resort gets a lot of drop-in business from experienced boaters who are heading up or down the Strait of Georgia, and repeat visitors often book up to a year in advance.

Accommodations in the nearby Parksville and Qualicum Beach

areas range from serviced campgrounds to luxury resorts, but since "No Vacancy" signs are a common sight along the Island Highway during the summer months, you should book early to avoid disappointment.

## Weather and Water Conditions

Parksville resident Dick Brune, former owner of the French Creek Store and Charters, guided for decades before retiring. And when he wasn't fishing with customers or friends, he was often sailing, so his knowledge of the area and its weather is unsurpassed. He advises that from November through January strong southeasters are common. These are fairly predictable as they build up slowly and you know that, once the whitecaps start increasing, it's time to head for home. But these winter southeasters usually pose less danger than summer northwesters, which might suddenly bring on rough water conditions despite sunny, clear blue skies.

If fishing for winter feeder chinooks, you can usually find action in some fairly protected areas around Ballenas Channel and Lasqueti Island, but pay close attention to the horizon. A dark wind line indicates worsening weather, and if it turns white, a northwester will probably appear within a half-hour—meaning it's time to head for cover immediately.

However, overall this area enjoys a moderate climate. April and May are fairly mild, June fluctuates between warm and chilly, and July through September is usually dependably nice except for unforeseen winds or fog, which start around early to mid-September. Early October can also be reasonable, but by November you can expect winter conditions to prevail until spring.

The French Creek Marina can become clogged with boats during the summer months.

As there are no major tide rips or fast-flowing currents in this area's nearshore waters, small boats work quite well, but for longer runs off-shore plan on something more suitable for the task.

## Run Timing

Feeder chinooks are available year round and fishing for them is popular throughout April and May. A few early migratory chinooks bound for the Fraser and its tributaries usually start appearing at some point during early June. Other southward migrations follow throughout the summer, most of which hold in the area for varying periods to feed on herring and needlefish. Most chinook fishing throughout June and July is for migratory stocks that are moving through; Qualicum Bay generally starts producing good action around the first week in August, especially off the Qualicum and Little Qualicum river mouths as local chinooks return.

When the hatchery coho retention season opens on July 1, they should average 6-8 pounds but they grow somewhat larger by September, with a few reaching double-digit weights. Pinks appear in late July and are most abundant during odd-numbered years. Local stocks are usually found close inshore where they provide a popular beach fishery.

Local migratory chinooks usually peak in early September, by which time they have been joined by northern coho that continue to provide good fishing until month's end. If the weather turns stormy during this period, the fishing might drop off but it always comes back on after a day or two. There are usually good chum returns starting in late September and a few continue running well into November.

Dan Siminiuk with a trophy chinook caught off French Creek.

## Hotspots and Tactics

Winter chinooks may be found anywhere from the Little Qualicum River mouth southeast to Nanoose Harbour and northward to Lasqueti Island. Check around the Nanoose Harbour mouth, Maude, Winchelsea,

Gerald and Ballenas islands, Cottam Point, Northwest Bay and French Creek. Weather permitting, Lasqueti, Sangster and Jenkins islands are worth a look.

When feeder chinooks scatter and the pickings get slim, anglers who produce good catches with any degree of consistency are those who keep current with where the fish have moved and are willing to put in long, hard days of fishing if need be. This might involve travelling over long distances to locate the action, which is when having a fast, seaworthy boat is appreciated. Fortunately, many local anglers make a point of exchanging information on the whereabouts of salmon schools, greatly reducing the time spent searching for them.

Feeder chinooks are usually present around Mistaken Island and Ballenas Channel, and Cottam Reef offers good drift-jigging opportunities. Some of the best chinook and coho trolling is located along the inshore shelf that runs from Brant Point to the Little Qualicum River, especially the stretch between the marina and Columbia Beach.

Early in the season, try downrigging with a chrome dodger trailing a red or pink hoochie on a 40-inch leader. As the season progresses and larger fish start feeding more heavily on baitfish, switch to a flasher with red or lime-green trim, trailing a 3-inch white or glow Hot Spot Apex trimmed with green or grey or a hoochie on a 36- to 42-inch leader. Good searching colours are green/white and blue/white. If you prefer bait with your flasher, use cut-plug, strip or whole herring in a teaser but extend the leader to 5 or 6 feet. Hoochies and drift-jigs also remain productive throughout these periods.

Glen Massick points out that 4-inch spoons can be productive from January until the herring spawn. Based on sales at his AGM Outdoorsman's Pit Stop in Parksville, he suggests trying two-tone Coyotes and Tomics in patterns like green/glow, green/white, blue/chrome and black/white. Trail them about 60 inches behind an O'Ki or Hot Spot flasher at 180 feet.

Timing of the Strait of Georgia herring spawn varies from year to year, but some period in March is usually a safe prediction. When it occurs, try trolling Tomic plugs or cut-plug herring that match the average bait size. This tactic usually continues working well throughout the spring, long after the spawn.

Lasqueti Island is surrounded by a rugged, irregular nearshore bottom structure plus several coves and smaller islands, all of which add up to good fishing prospects. While these can be very productive areas, because the uneven bottom comes up fast, it pays to monitor your depth sounder closely. Certainly worth a look in May is the western end of Lasqueti from Prowse Point below False Bay and then around past the Finnerty Islands to the Fegan Islets and the area around Jenkins Island.

Downrigging right off French Creek should also continue to produce well in May. Once out of the harbour, troll northwest along the 50-metre contour line toward the Little Qualicum River mouth then back again to either French Creek or beyond to Brant Point. If you don't find any action on the first run, try going out a bit deeper on subsequent passes. This can be productive during low light conditions such as late evenings.

Drift-jigging is popular here, especially at dusk off Columbia Beach between the marina and Qualicum Beach. Other productive spots are along the drop-off at Elephant Eye Point on the eastern end of Sangster Island, Jenkins Island and the Sisters Islets off the western end of Lasqueti Island. Various lures work but the most popular are Zzingers, Buzz Bombs and Pirkens in pink pearl or white with a trim of green, black, blue or pink.

During July and August it's often possible to find some good action at the north end of Lasqueti Island by fishing close to shore with plug-cut or large herring strip. At the south end try trolling back and forth from Bull Passage to Young Point. Start at the 60-metre shelf then move out to the 90-metre contour line and fish deep. Large fish like to hang out on the edge of the shelves. Trolling Tomic plugs is often productive and drift-jigging can really turn on at times. Chinook success usually hinges on the right combination of light conditions, water depth and tidal flow.

Jill Stefanyk with a dandy chinook caught while fishing with her father, Larry, out of French Creek.

This is the period when the southeastern side of Lasqueti Island attracts considerable attention, especially around Sangster Island, Seal Rock and Poor Man's Rock. The large reef extending eastward from Lasqueti gets extremely popular at times. In addition to local anglers you may often see large party boats that have made the run over from Vancouver and, if there is an opening, commercial fishing vessels as well. While thoughts of fishing in such crowded conditions might not seem appealing, just pause to consider why so many anglers gather there so consistently—and then join in the fun. When local migratory chinooks move into the area, they often favour the 16- to 40-metre contour line bordering the eastern Vancouver Island shoreline, but during early morning twilight those same fish might be found feeding actively in water as shallow as 10 feet.

When northern coho are present, early morning bucktailing can produce some exciting fishing. Proven patterns are Green Hornet (dark green back, white belly), Green Ghost (fluorescent green back, white belly), Grey Ghost (grey back, white belly), Moby Dick (all white) and Saratoga (mid-green back, white belly). While bucktails can be fished with or without a spinner in front, most anglers feel that a whirling blade increases a fly's visibility and creates sound that is also an attractant. Blades of white abalone shell (mother-of-pearl) between the size of a nickel and a quarter are favoured, usually in a rounded Colorado shape. Metal blades also work, either in smooth or hammered silver or gold or a painted surface of fluorescent green or red. If a sinker is required, make it as light as possible. Keel-shaped bead chain sinkers of

up to 1¼-ounces work well, but for heavier weights use a slip sinker clipped about 15 feet ahead of the swivel. Coho are attracted to bucktails moving in an erratic path, so swerve your boat from side to side, causing the outside flies to constantly speed up and slow down.

Flat-line trolling with plugs is popular off the river mouths, usually with a 4- to 6-inch Tomic in shades of white or pink pearl trimmed with green, blue or grey trailed up to 50 feet behind a 2- to

Trolling a fly right on the surface in a boat's wake is an exciting—and often productive—way to fish for coho (and chinooks).

Most anglers fishing out of French Creek rely on exchanging information in order to keep track of where salmon schools are located.

16-ounce slip sinker for maximum action. Downriggers are also an option as is drift-jigging.

NOTE: there are fishing closures off the mouths of the Qualicum and Little Qualicum rivers from August 25 to October 15, so check the regulations for details.

## AVAILABLE MARINE CHARTS

3512 Strait of Georgia, Central Portion
3463 Strait of Georgia, Southern Portion

### Marine Chart Coordinates:

| Place Names: | | Place Names: | |
|---|---|---|---|
| Ballenas Channel | LAT 49°20' LONG 124°10' | Little Qualicum River | LAT 49°22' LONG 124°30' |
| Brant Point | LAT 49°19' LONG 124°16' | Mistaken Island | LAT 49°20' LONG 124°13' |
| Columbia Beach | LAT 49°21' LONG 124°23' | Parksville | LAT 49°19' LONG 124°19' |
| Cottam Reef | LAT 49°19' LONG 124°11' | Prowse Point | LAT 49°29' LONG 124°21' |
| Elephant Eye Point | LAT 49°26' LONG 124°12' | Poor Man's Rock | LAT 49°26' LONG 124°10' |
| False Bay | LAT 49°29' LONG 124°21' | Qualicum Beach | LAT 49°21' LONG 124°27' |
| Fegan Islets | LAT 49°32' LONG 124°23' | Sangster Island | LAT 49°26' LONG 124°12' |
| Finnerty Islands | LAT 49°30' LONG 124°24' | Scottie Bay | LAT 49°31' LONG 124°21' |
| French Creek Marina | LAT 49°21' LONG 124°21' | Seal Reef | LAT 49°26' LONG 124°14' |
| Jenkins Island | LAT 49°27' LONG 124°18' | Sisters Islets | LAT 49°29' LONG 124°26' |
| Lasqueti Island | LAT 49°29' LONG 124°16' | | |

# Nanaimo to Schooner Cove

Nanaimo—the Hub City—is probably best known for its BC Ferries terminal, which accounts for thousands of vehicles passing through this city of 62,000 on a daily basis. From late spring until early fall, many of these cars contain anglers intent on driving to saltwater fishing destinations much farther afield. Some, however, remain in the area, knowing they are already amid good salmon fishing opportunities.

Looking out toward the Strait of Georgia from the Charlaine Boat Ramp at the northern end of Nanaimo.

## Our Information Sources

Russ Bartrim, owner, Vi-Dean Charters, Parksville
Pat Johnson, former owner, Sealand Tackle
Bill Martin, owner, Smoothy Charters, Parksville

## For visitor information:

NANAIMO VISITOR INFO CENTRE
Beban House
2290 Bowen Road
Nanaimo, BC V9T 3K7
800-663-7337
(250) 756-0075
info@tourismanaimo.com
www.tourismnanaimo.com

Family members or friends not inclined toward fishing can enjoy time on Nanaimo's various golf courses, go wildlife viewing, book a sailing charter, do some horseback riding, or simply indulge in a bit of casual beachcombing. The more adventuresome might try river or ocean kayaking, mountaineering, scuba diving, spelunking in the area's many caves or even go bungee jumping. Whatever their choices, when evening arrives those with time on their hands might consider visiting one of the city's outstanding concert halls, theatres or nightclubs. Other "non-fishing" pastimes worth considering are visiting the Nanaimo District Museum and The Bastion (the last remaining fort of its kind in North America), taking the short ferry ride to Newcastle Island Provincial Park or popping in for a beer at the Dinghy Dock, Canada's only floating pub.

Accommodations are not a problem. Visitors may choose from a wide range of hotels, motels, resorts, bed and breakfast operations and campgrounds. In addition, as well as providing berths for local boats, several marinas handle the increased transient marine traffic that

The Dinghy Dock is a floating pub off the Nanaimo waterfront.

occurs during the summer months. Although some are full all year, most operate on a first-come, first-served basis.

If you are trailering your own boat, the largest and easiest ramp to use is the City of Nanaimo Brechin Boat Launch, located right beside the Departure Bay Ferry Terminal. There are also ramps at the north end of town at the City of Nanaimo Charlaine Boat Launch and to the south at Cedar by the Sea Boat Launch. Ramps in the Nanoose Bay area are located at the Beachcomber Marina (1600 Brynmarl Road) and Fairwinds Schooner Cove Resort & Marina (3521 Dolphin Drive).

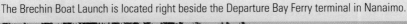

The Brechin Boat Launch is located right beside the Departure Bay Ferry terminal in Nanaimo.

## Weather and Water Conditions

Nanaimo enjoys mild winters with slightly less precipitation than Vancouver. Spring, summer and fall are generally moderate and July, August and September are relatively free of rain. Like all open-water locations, the stretch from Nanaimo to Ballenas Channel, about 25 km northwest, is subject to variable weather conditions. From November to January strong southeasters are common, but those with seaworthy boats often find fishable water behind the islands clustered in Ballenas Channel. The use of caution and common sense is strongly recommended as is close monitoring of VHF radios for warnings of worsening weather. The fairly predictable winter winds usually pose less danger than summer northwesters, which suddenly develop rough water conditions despite sunny, clear blue skies.

## Run Timing

Born and raised on Vancouver Island, Robert Van Pelt started guiding at age 16 and has since worked within the recreational fishing industry in wholesale and retail sales. An avid promoter of the Nanaimo area's saltwater fishing opportunities, Van Pelt maintains that, with good local populations of feeder chinooks, year-round fishing is available to those willing to put in the time and effort. Much of November is usually a write-off both because of bad weather and the fact that a high percentage of chinooks at this time of year are shakers under the 62-cm-long limit. By December legal fish averaging 8 or 9 pounds are present in fair numbers, but they are scattered so you must search for them.

While a few early migratory chinooks bound for the Fraser and its tributaries

Robert Van Pelt with a typical feeder chinook from the Five Finger Island area off Nanaimo

might appear around early June, the heavy runs don't usually show until late June to early July. Those early fish average in the 20-pound range but 30 pounds or more are possible. These southward migrations continue in varying densities throughout the summer, with the action appearing wherever the schools concentrate to feed on the baitfish.

When hatchery-marked coho open for retention, they should probably average 4 to 6 pounds, but by September fish of 10 to 14 pounds are distinct possibilities. Pink salmon usually show up in early August and provide excellent inshore and beach fishing. They are most abundant during odd-numbered years. Chums start arriving in September but attract relatively little attention because anglers are still intent on chinooks and late-running northern coho.

## Hotspots and Tactics

WARNING: while fishing in or around the mouth of Departure Bay or in any of BC Ferries' lanes, ferries always have the right-of-way. Never try arguing this point because you won't ever win.

Tide conditions are important to fishing in this area, so a current tide table is important. In addition, many high-liners and fishing guides rely on John Alden Knight's *Solunar Tables*, claiming it gives them an edge at monitoring major and minor changes in feeding patterns. It's hard to argue with success.

As winter fishing action moves to wherever the baitfish are congregating, you might find yourself heading northwest toward Ballenas Channel or southeast into the Gulf Islands. Nevertheless, many of the best-known fishing areas are right off the Nanaimo waterfront, and the fact that they get a fair amount of year-round angling pressure indicates that the overall catch rate must make it worthwhile.

Feeder chinooks are usually scattered from October through December, but fish up to 15-plus pounds can be found around Entrance Island, Hudson Rock and Five Finger Island. In December you will also find them around Snake Island, Neck Point, "The Brickyard," Horswell Bluff and Clarke Rock. The waters around Snake Island are most popular because they are always dependable for chinooks and then coho later in the year. Be warned, however, that the red buoy on the south side marks a very shallow point. Other popular spots include Horswell Channel, the "White Marker," Departure Bay, Rainbow Channel, Orlebar Point, Northumberland Channel, Newcastle Island, Nanaimo Harbour and "The Grande," which is marked by a large log building on

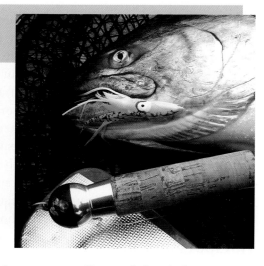

As green and white hoochies account for a lot of salmon each season, they are a standard searching pattern.

the bluffs about 500 metres west of the northwest entrance to Silva Bay.

The Ballenas Islands area is best for feeder chinooks on the west side along the 40-metre edges. Mistaken Island is usually dependable year round, and Cottam Reef—easily identified by the spar buoy between Dorcas Point and Dorcas Rock—is especially good for drift-jigging as baitfish are usually close to the reef. Trollers should try between the reef and Mistaken Island.

One of the most popular early-season chinook lures is the venerable green/white hoochie 34 inches behind a silver or chrome Hot Spot flasher, but don't overlook other colour combinations like green glow, purple haze, blood-and-bones, and Moby Dick. Those using bait favour anchovies or fairly small whole herring in clear, clear/green or army truck Rhys Davis Anchovy Specials, herring strip in a green or clear Rhys Davis teaser or a small cut-plug herring. Spoons are an option, especially Coyotes or Tomics in cop car, army truck and glow green. Whichever bait is used, trail it about 6 feet behind a clear plaid, purple haze or green/silver Hot Spot flasher. For spoons, shorten the leader by a foot.

Try downrigging at depths between 150 and 180 feet. Once fish are located, continue trolling or switch to mooching or drift-jigging. These tactics also pay off when chinooks are feeding near the surface during early mornings and tide changes. As the season progresses there are few changes in trolling techniques other than increasing the bait or lure size to match the baitfish and switching to flashers with green or red trim. If chinooks are feeding on herring, virtually any size of fresh bait attracts them, but if targeting needlefish in closer to shore, they often become quite size specific. Small herring strips trimmed to match the size of the needlefish will usually turn the trick.

Tomic plugs can be productive. The most popular "general purpose" model is a no. 191 with a green back and black scale finish. A 3-inch model works well for winter fish, but as the season progresses they prefer plugs 4 to 6 inches long and often become colour selective. The no. 191 should continue producing but the 158, 203 and 602 also come into their own.

Chinook fishing continues on through June, by which time you might be trying anywhere from 1.5 to 8 km offshore around Five Finger Island and Thrasher Rock and inshore from "The Grande" to Whalebone Point, Orlebar Point to Tinson Point and around Neck Point. Good lure choices are an anchovy in a Rhys Davis Anchovy Special, various spoons and green/glow white splatterback hoochies trolled at depths of 90 to 150 feet. Typical leader lengths are 6 feet when used with bait, 5 feet with spoons, and 3½ feet with hoochies.

Drift-jigging with Buzz Bombs or Zzingers picks up in June, especially around Hudson Rock, Five Finger Island, Orlebar Point, Entrance Reef and Thrasher Rock. Some impressive chinooks have been landed by anglers casting from shore at Neck Point where the reef ends abruptly and the bottom drops quickly away to a depth that attracts them. Once the coho season opens for retention, try a variety of spoons, Hot Spot Apex, squirts or a small herring strip in an action head. Shorten your leaders down to 42 to 48 inches and troll slightly faster than for chinooks.

July and August usually produce some chinooks to 35 pounds off Whalebone Point, "The Cannery," Five Finger Island and Neck Point. Good trolling depths usually range from 60 to 80 feet at dawn and dusk and down to 180 feet during daylight hours.

All islands in the Ballenas Channel area are surrounded by rocks and reefs, so carry a marine chart on board and monitor your depth sounder closely. This area offers year-round fishing but the peak "overall" period is from early April to late September. For the most part, feeder chinooks favour the western sides of the islands, rocks and reefs, but bait availability and the height and flow of tidal currents can alter their feeding depths and preferences, often quite dramatically. Because this area is carpeted with tackle-grabbing shallows, adjust your tactics accordingly. Moochers using live herring, cut-plug or strip should do well along the drop-offs and in deeper waters. For working in close to and over the tops of the various reefs, try drift-jigging, casting lures, and bucktailing. Fly casting out around the islands has become increasingly popular for coho.

Try trolling for coho between Gerald and Douglas islands and the surrounding reefs or between Douglas and Amelia islands. Coho often move in close to the Yeo Islands, but chinooks favour the deep water on the Ballenas Channel side. The Winchelsea Islands are fairly dependable for chinooks, then large coho later in the year. Fish right around all of the islands, including southward to the Ada Islands and eastward to Grey Rock, Rudder Rock and Edgell Banks. The reefs around Ruth and Southey islands are quite shallow, but if bait moves onto the shoals, the drop-offs can provide good action on drift-jigs. Maud Island and the entrance to Nanoose Harbour can be very productive, as can the shallow reef running northeast from Fleet Point past Blunden and Icarus points to Neck Point. Although chinooks may be found anywhere along the bordering drop-offs, fishing is usually best around one or more of the points. Don't overlook drift-jigging just at sunset around the Winchelsea Islands, Grey Rock, the reef outside Gerald Island and the Ballenas Islands as this can be especially productive. For late-running pinks and early chums try trolling shallower—40 to 100 feet—and at slower speeds with a red Hot Spot flasher and a small pink hoochie on a 24- to 26-inch leader.

September usually offers chinook and coho fishing around Porlier Pass, Thrasher Rock and "The Grande" to Whalebone Point, around Entrance Reef, Orlebar Point to Pilot Bay, around Snake Island, Five Finger Island, Neck and Icarus points. The "Brickyard," about midway between Neck and Icarus points, is popular with trollers and drift-jiggers alike. This is the time to downrig at 80 to 180 feet with an anchovy or strip in a clear/green scale Rhys Davis teaser, spoons in green/white or black/white, and green splatterback hoochies. Also productive are 5- and 6-inch no. 191, 158, 203 and 602 Tomic plugs, but once the last of the big migratory chinooks have gone upstream, usually by early October, drop back down to the 3-inchers if you want to attract those feeders.

203 Tomic Plug

## AVAILABLE MARINE CHARTS

3310 Gulf Islands (Victoria Harbour to Nanaimo Harbour)
3457 Nanaimo Harbour and Departure Bay
3458 Approaches to Nanaimo Harbour
3459 Approaches to Nanoose Harbour
3512 Strait of Georgia, Central Portion
3463 Strait of Georgia, Southern Portion

### Marine Chart Coordinates:

| Place Names: | | Place Names: | |
|---|---|---|---|
| Ada Islands | LAT 49°17' LONG 124°05' | Maud Island | LAT 49°16' LONG 124°05' |
| Amelia Island | LAT 49°18' LONG 124°09' | Mistaken Island | LAT 49°20' LONG 124°13' |
| Ballenas Channel | LAT 49°20' LONG 124°10' | Nanaimo Harbour | LAT 49°10' LONG 123°54' |
| Ballenas Islands | LAT 49°21' LONG 124°09' | Nanaimo | LAT 49°10' LONG 123°56' |
| Blunden Point | LAT 49°15' LONG 124°05' | Nanoose Bay | LAT 49°16' LONG 124°12' |
| "Brickyard" | LAT 49°14' LONG 124°00' | Nanoose Harbour | LAT 49°16' LONG 124°10' |
| Clarke Rock | LAT 49°13' LONG 123°56' | Neck Point | LAT 49°14' LONG 123°58' |
| Cottam Reef | LAT 49°19' LONG 124°11' | Newcastle Island | LAT 49°11' LONG 123°56' |
| Departure Bay | LAT 49°12' LONG 123°58' | Northumberland Channel | LAT 49°09' LONG 123°51' |
| Dorcas Point | LAT 49°19' LONG 124°11' | Orlebar Point | LAT 49°12' LONG 123°49' |
| Dorcas Rock | LAT 49°19' LONG 124°11' | Pilot Bay | LAT 49°12' LONG 123°51' |
| Douglas Island | LAT 49°19' LONG 124°09' | Porlier Pass | LAT 49°01' LONG 123°35' |
| Edgell Banks | LAT 49°16' LONG 124°03' | Rainbow Channel | LAT 49°14' LONG 123°53' |
| Entrance Island | LAT 49°13' LONG 123°48' | Rudder Rock | LAT 49°17' LONG 124°04' |
| Five Finger Island | LAT 49°14' LONG 123°55' | Ruth Island | LAT 49°18' LONG 124°08' |
| Fleet Point | LAT 49°15' LONG 124°08' | Schooner Cove | LAT 49°04' LONG 124°48' |
| Gabriola Island | LAT 49°10' LONG 123°48' | Silva Bay | LAT 49°09' LONG 123°42' |
| Gerald Island | LAT 49°19' LONG 124°10' | Snake Island | LAT 49°13' LONG 123°53' |
| "The Grande" | LAT 49°09' LONG 123°42' | Southey Island | LAT 49°17' LONG 124°06' |
| Grey Rock | LAT 49°17' LONG 124°04' | Thrasher Rock | LAT 49°09' LONG 123°39' |
| Horswell Channel | LAT 49°13' LONG 123°56' | Tinson Point | LAT 49°12' LONG 123°51' |
| Horswell Bluff | LAT 49°13' LONG 123°56' | Whalebone Point | LAT 49°56' LONG 124°48' |
| Hudson Rocks | LAT 49°13' LONG 123°55' | Winchelsea Islands | LAT 49°18' LONG 124°05' |
| Icarus Point | LAT 49°15' LONG 124°02' | Yeo Islands | LAT 49°18' LONG 124°08' |
| Lantzville | LAT 49°15' LONG 124°04' | | |

# Gulf Islands

Stretching about 60 kilometres along the southeastern shoreline of Vancouver Island—between Nanaimo and Sidney—is a meandering maze of over 200 islands, islets and channels known as the Gulf Islands. It is the most beautiful and interesting area in which to fish or cruise to be found within the Strait of Georgia. Here you may experience ever-changing panoramas that include gently sloping sandy beaches; craggy, lichen-covered cliffs; stately, lush-green evergreens interspersed with

the twisted, reddish-brown trunks of arbutus trees; rolling, grassy farmland dotted with flocks of sheep; vast booming grounds filled with logs
destined for nearby pulp mills and sawmills; and docks surrounded by
everything from commercial fishing boats and tugs to dinky little dories
and some truly awesome ocean-going yachts.

The population consists of people who work on the islands or com-
mute elsewhere—many of them part-timers who maintain homes here
that they can visit whenever time permits—plus legions of retirees.
Most of the destinations covered elsewhere in this book have one major
point of entry, but the Gulf Islands have several. Lower Mainland
anglers with fast, seaworthy boats can reach the outer Gulf Islands by
open water crossings of about 35 km from Vancouver or 20 km from

## Our Information Sources

Terry Gjernes, retired DFO fisheries biologist
Kim Zak, independent fishing guide

## For visitor information:

**CHEMAINUS VISITOR CENTRE**
9796 Willow Street
Box 575
Chemainus, BC V0R 1K0
(250) 246-3944
www.chemainus.bc.ca

**DUNCAN VISITOR CENTRE**
381A Trans-Canada Highway
Duncan, BC V9L 3R5
(250) 748-1111
(888) 303-3337
www.duncan.bc.ca

**GALIANO ISLAND TOURIST/VISITOR INFO**
2590 Sturdies Bay Road (July 1- August 31)
Box 73
Galiano Island, BC V0N 1P0
(250) 539-2233
(866) 539-2233
(250) 539-2507 (Off season)
www.galianoisland.com

**LADYSMITH TOURIST/VISITOR INFO**
132C Roberts Street
Box 98
Ladysmith, BC V9G 1A4
(250) 245-2112
www.ladysmithcofc.com

**NANAIMO VISITOR CENTRE**
Beban House
2290 Bowen Road
Nanaimo, BC V9T 3K7
(250) 756-0106
(800) 663-7337
www.tourismnanaimo.com

**SALTSPRING ISLAND VISITOR CENTRE**
121 Lower Ganges Road
Ganges, BC V8K 2T1
(250) 537-5252
(866) 216-2936
www.saltspringtoday.com

**SOUTH COWICHAN TOURIST/VISITOR INFO**
Mill Bay Centre (May 18-September 4)
2720 Mill Bay Road
Mill Bay, BC V0R 2P1
(250) 743-3566
info@southcowichanchamber.org

Anglers cruising and fishing in the Gulf Island area will experience some of the most beautiful and interesting scenery found within the Strait of Georgia.

Tsawwassen. The Vancouver Island access points to the Gulf Islands are Nanaimo, Ladysmith, Chemainus, Crofton, Maple Bay, Duncan (Cowichan Bay), Mill Bay and Sidney plus Ganges and Fulford Harbour on Saltspring Island. All locations offer varying ranges of accommodations and amenities, so anglers may select whichever destination is closest to where they plan to fish.

## Weather and Water Conditions

The claim by Gulf Islands promoters to having a Mediterranean climate might be just a wee bit exaggerated, but the islands certainly do enjoy mild winters and warm, dry summer weather that hovers around 25 degrees Celsius. The monthly average for the southern islands from May through September is over 250 hours of sunshine and less than 3 cm of rain. The northern Gulf Islands aren't quite as warm or dry but the differences are minor.

Winds seldom create problems inside the island cluster, but outside waters are subject to the prevailing Strait of Georgia winds and storms. From November to January strong southeasters are common, but fishable water can often be found in the lee of an island. Boaters crossing the Strait of Georgia between the Lower Mainland and Gulf Islands must maintain a sharp watch for summer northwesters, which develop quickly despite clear blue skies. Late summer fog is also a fact of life. Combined with the profusion of islands, this can cause major confusion for boaters who are not prepared with a reliable compass and marine chart and—better yet—a Global Positioning System.

Most waters are safe for small boats with the notable exceptions being Active Pass, Nose Point in Captain Passage, Gabriola Passage, Race Point in Porlier Pass and Dodd Narrows in Northumberland Channel. All of these develop swift currents and rough water conditions during peak tidal flows.

## Run Timing

Virtually all areas within the Gulf Islands produce good fishing at times but a few are more dependable than others and are, therefore, more popular and crowded. Several areas offer year-round fishing for resident feeder chinooks. During the fall months a high percentage are shakers under the 62-cm-long limit, but by December some are averaging 8 or 9 pounds. Large migratory chinooks usually appear in February and remain in the area until mid- to late October.

Some areas experience excellent coho action from August through early December, occasionally later, but the overall peak is usually late September to late October. Pink salmon usually show in August and chums in September.

## Hotspots and Tactics

Fishing for feeder and migratory chinooks is generally quiet until November but often quite good by February and March. There are lots of protected waters from which to choose, but some of the more productive ones include Porlier Pass, Active Pass, Sansum Narrows, Bold Bluff Point, Flat Top Islands, Thrasher Rock and Ladysmith Harbour. In the Chemainus area try off Bare Point and around Hospital Rock and Bird Rock at Hospital Point. Crofton usually has good winter and spring

chinook fishing near the pulp mill outfall, an area that lends itself to mooching or drift-jigging. Also work the shoreline from Sherard Point past Grave Point to Arbutus Point. For early season chinooks, try trolling or downrigging with a green/yellow, green glow, jellyfish or purple haze flasher. Six feet behind, trail an anchovy in a green, glow or jellyfish Anchovy Special teaser, cut-plug or

Bob Meyer with a 32-pound chinook caught off Thrasher Rock. *Silver Blue Charters photo*

strip, the latter with or without a green or clear Rhys Davis Large Teaser. Hootchies, squirts and spoons can also be productive—try army truck, cop car, green glow or purple haze. Colour does make a difference here, so if what you are using isn't working, don't hesitate to change colours.

The inside waters of Active Pass are relatively protected from off-shore winds. Common sense dictates that anglers avoid the ferry lanes, but there is often good winter chinook fishing in Miners Bay, well out of harm's way. Other spots to consider are close in to Mary Anne Point, Helen Point, Village Bay and around Enterprise Reef.

As the season progresses, use increasingly larger herring, hoochies or spoons, and switch to flashers with green/gold, purple or blue trim. If needlefish are present, the salmon can be quite fussy, but herring strips trimmed to match the needlefish in size and shape will often turn the trick. Downrigging with plugs is also a good bet. Trailing a plug without a flasher 40 to 80 feet behind the cannonball will ensure its maximum swimming action. Popular models include Tomic in white, pink pearl or chrome trimmed with green, blue, black or grey. Start out with 3-inch models for feeder chinooks, but as the season progresses and migratory fish start arriving, work up to 6 inches.

For mooching or motor-mooching with live or cut-plug herring, use a long, limber rod and a single-action reel loaded with a minimum of 300 yards of 15- to 25-pound-test nylon monofilament. Terminal rigging should consist of a 1½- to 4-ounce keel sinker, a leader at least 8 feet in length and a tandem hook setup.

Drift-jigging can be quite productive, especially in some of the shallower reef-filled areas or along the steep drop-offs that chinooks favour. Salmon can be very particular about the size, colour and action of a lure, so rather than filling your tackle box with a variety of different lures, concentrate on a few brands in a wide range of sizes and colours and then learn how to rig and use them properly. Local knowledge as to brands, colours, depths and techniques are key to your success when drift-jigging. Consult with a local tackle shop to determine what's working and don't hesitate to ask other anglers—most are willing to share this sort of information.

If salmon are running deep, a good searching method is to downrig just off the bottom while closely monitoring the depth sounder so the cannonballs can be raised and lowered accordingly. At the same time watch for concentrations of bait that usually attract chinooks. Once located, they can often be caught by mooching or drift-jigging.

Once the coho season opens, try trolling with a flasher and a Hot Spot Apex, Ross Swimmertail, Krippled K or Tom Mack. Some locations lend themselves well to bucktailing, especially during early morning and evening periods when the surface is relatively calm but slightly wind-rippled. Match the fly sizes and colours to the bait present, which includes herring, needlefish and shiner seaperch, meaning fairly large patterns that incorporate white with black or shades of green, blue, grey or purple. Casting and spinning with small spoons is becoming increasingly popular as is fly casting. Simply drift along the shoreline with the motor off and cast toward shore.

Because the Gulf Islands are so accessible from the Lower Mainland and southern Vancouver Island, they attract large numbers of anglers. As a result, there is currently a permanent summer/fall closure on Cowichan Bay and seasonal spot closures in Active Pass, Porlier Pass, Yellow Point, Northumberland Channel, the Chemainus River mouth and Satellite Channel. This means that you must read the regulations carefully before making any plans. However, these closures have forced anglers to fish in these areas during the winter, spring and early summer with the result that they discovered a good run of migratory chinooks from February to late May/early June. These fish, ranging from 10 to 35 pounds, follow the feed, which means they are usually found travelling anywhere from 10 to 30 feet off the bottom. Find the feed and you will find the chinooks.

The Flat Top Islands at the southeastern end of Gabriola Island are good for feeder chinooks from April through September. Try along the seaward side of the drop-off, northeast to Brant Reef and over to Thrasher Rock at the northern end of Gabriola Reefs. Mooch or jig inside Thrasher Rock and Gabriola Reefs or troll the outside toward Gabriola Passage. This is also a good area after the coho opening.

To the southeast, along the outer shore of Valdes Island, is Porlier Pass (known locally as "The Gap"), the most popular fishing area in the Gulf Islands. Coho usually show up in March and are available through September. Good bets are the bell buoy at the eastern entrance, the Georgia Strait side during flood tides and the Trincomali Channel side on ebbs. Note that tidal currents in Porlier reach 16 km/h creating rough water and whirlpools, especially around Race Point.

Dodd Narrows and Round Island at the lower end of Northumberland Channel are spotty for coho during late summer and fall but good for chinooks in late August. Yellow Point and Thetis

Island offer good chinooks from December through May, then they slow down until September. Coho can be excellent after the opening and should remain fair to good through October. Try eastward from Yellow Point to Miami Islet, southwest to Fraser Point on Thetis Island (watch for the reef at the midway point) then northwest across to Deer Point. At the northwestern tip of Thetis Island, fish along the reef running from Pilkey Point past the Ragged Islets and Miami Island right on up to Danger Reefs. Depending on tidal flow, troll or jig along the reef's "downstream" side.

At Kuper Island, try from Donckele Point in Telegraph Cove, southward past Active Point, Augustus Point, Tent Island and around North Reef. Heading northwest, stay outside of the reef surrounding Sandstone Rocks and continue up Houstoun Channel to Josling Point. Also try from Telegraph Cove toward Hudson Island then swing around Alarm Rock toward Dayman and Scott islands.

The Ladysmith area is fairly good for feeder chinooks from December to April and for larger fish through spring and summer. In Ladysmith Harbour try between Dunsmuir Island and Holland Bank. Other hotspots are south between Coffin and Boulder points or north from Sharpe Point past Coffin Point and Kulleet Bay to Yellow Point, but watch for shallow reefs between Sharpe Point and Nares Rock.

Around Chemainus try for chinooks—and coho later on—along the shoreline from Bare Point past Boulder Point to Davis Lagoon. From Maple Bay, try between Maxwell Point and Burgoyne Bay or southeast along the shoreline from Paddy Mile Stone to Octopus Point then down to Sansum Narrows, which has good winter chinooks around Bold Bluff Point from January to early April. Migratory chinooks start appearing in late February and continue travelling through this area until late May. Large chinooks usually arrive in the Narrows during July and remain until September. This fishery generally lasts from dawn to mid-morning. Although coho start showing in August, the peak is generally from mid-September through late October and often well into November. Coho favour the Saltspring Island side of the Narrows, with the best action at either end, depending on the tide. From Separation Point, try along the shoreline past the mouth of Genoa Bay up to and around Sansum Point. Keep close to shore as it drops steeply. Chinooks and coho favour the deep water just inside the point. Also try around Burial Islet and southward down Satellite Channel to Boatswain Bank off Cherry Point.

Gibbs Nortac Wonder Spoon 50/50
brass and nickel.

Active Pass is subject
to heavy ferry traffic, and
the Strait of Georgia side
receives prevailing off-
shore winds plus some
rough tide rips during tide changes. Outside of the entrance try
Georgina Shoals and what is known locally as the "Ladder Hole" just
off the Georgina Point lighthouse. Other hotspots are around David
Cove, Gossip Shoals off Gossip Island and across the mouth of Whaler
Bay to Lion Islets.

Along the southwestern side of Galiano Island try between
Collinson Point and the mouth of Montague Harbour, keeping inside
the navigation light on Ben Mohr Rock. On Saturna Island, East Point
offers year-round chinooks and good coho prospects, but it can be
weather-controlled by the prevailing winds. Try close to shore from East
Point along the mouth of Narvaez Bay to Monarch Head. Tumbo Reef
and Rosenfeld Rock are also good bets.

## AVAILABLE MARINE CHARTS

3310 Gulf Islands—Victoria Harbour to Nanaimo Harbour
3441 Haro Strait, Boundary Pass and Satellite Channel
3442 North Pender Island to Thetis Island
3443 Thetis Island to Nanaimo
3458 Approaches to Nanaimo Harbour
3462 Juan de Fuca Strait to Strait of Georgia
3463 Strait of Georgia, Southern Portion
3475 Plans: Stuart Channel, Chemainus Bay, Ladysmith Harbour,
Dodd Narrows to Flat Top Islands, Dodd Narrows, Osborn Bay
3476 Approaches to Tsehum Harbour
3477 Plans—Gulf Islands: Bedwell Harbour to Georgeson Passage,
Telegraph Harbour and Preedy Harbour, Pender Canal
3478 Plans—Saltspring Island: Cowichan Bay to Maple Bay, Birds Eye
Cove, Genoa Bay, Ganges Harbour and Long Harbour, Fulford
Harbour

## Marine Chart Coordinates:

| Place Names: | | Place Names: | |
|---|---|---|---|
| Active Pass | LAT 48°53' LONG 123°18' | Kuper Island | LAT 48°58' LONG 123°39' |
| Active Point | LAT 48°57' LONG 123°40' | "Ladder Hole" | LAT 48°52' LONG 123°17' |
| Alarm Rock | LAT 48°57' LONG 123°41' | Ladysmith | LAT 48°59' LONG 123°49' |
| Arbutus Point | LAT 48°49' LONG 123°35' | Ladysmith Harbour | LAT 49°00' LONG 123°48' |
| Augustus Point | LAT 48°57' LONG 123°39' | Lion Islets | LAT 48°54' LONG 123°20' |
| Bare Point | LAT 48°56' LONG 123°42' | Maple Bay | LAT 48°49' LONG 123°36' |
| Ben Mohr Rock | LAT 48°51' LONG 123°23' | Mary Anne Point | LAT 48°52' LONG 123°19' |
| Bird Rock | LAT 48°56' LONG 123°43' | Maxwell Point | LAT 48°49' LONG 123°34' |
| Boatswain Bank | LAT 48°42' LONG 123°33' | Miami Islet | LAT 49°02' LONG 123°42' |
| Bold Bluff Point | LAT 48°47' LONG 123°33' | Mill Bay | LAT 48°39' LONG 123°33' |
| Boulder Point | LAT 48°23' LONG 123°58' | Miners Bay | LAT 48°51' LONG 123°18' |
| Brant Reef | LAT 49°10' LONG 124°40' | Monarch Head | LAT 48°46' LONG 123°06' |
| Burgoyne Bay | LAT 48°48' LONG 123°32' | Montague Harbour | LAT 48°53' LONG 123°24' |
| Burial Islet | LAT 48°46' LONG 123°34' | Nanaimo | LAT 49°10' LONG 123°56' |
| Captain Passage | LAT 48°49' LONG 123°24' | Nares Rock | LAT 49°59' LONG 123°45' |
| Chemainus | LAT 48°55' LONG 123°43' | Narvaez Bay | LAT 48°46' LONG 123°06' |
| Cherry Point | LAT 48°43' LONG 123°33' | North Reef | LAT 48°55' LONG 123°38' |
| Coffin Point | LAT 48°59' LONG 123°45' | Northumberland Channel | LAT 49°09' LONG 123°51' |
| Collinson Point | LAT 48°52' LONG 123°21' | Nose Point | LAT 48°51' LONG 123°25' |
| Crofton | LAT 48°52' LONG 123°39' | Octopus Point | LAT 48°48' LONG 123°34' |
| Danger Reefs | LAT 49°03' LONG 123°43' | Osborn Bay | LAT 48°52' LONG 123°38' |
| David Cove | LAT 48°51' LONG 123°16' | Paddy Mile Stone | LAT 48°49' LONG 123°25' |
| Davis Lagoon | LAT 48°57' LONG 123°46' | Pilkey Point | LAT 49°01' LONG 123°41' |
| Dayman Island | LAT 48°58' LONG 123°41' | Porlier Pass | LAT 49°01' LONG 123°35' |
| Deer Point | LAT 49°02' LONG 123°46' | Race Point | LAT 49°01' LONG 123°35' |
| Dodd Narrows | LAT 49°08' LONG 123°49' | Ragged Islets | LAT 49°23' LONG 123°27' |
| Donckele Point | LAT 48°58' LONG 123°40' | Rosenfeld Rock | LAT 48°48' LONG 123°02' |
| Duncan | LAT 48°47' LONG 123°42' | Round Island | LAT 49°07' LONG 123°48' |
| Dunsmuir Islands | LAT 48°59' LONG 123°47' | Saltspring Island | LAT 48°45' LONG 123°29' |
| East Point | LAT 48°47' LONG 123°03' | Sandstone Rocks | LAT 48°55' LONG 123°37' |
| Enterprise Reef | LAT 48°51' LONG 123°21' | Sansum Narrows | LAT 48°48' LONG 123°34' |
| Flat Top Islands | LAT 49°09' LONG 123°41' | Satellite Channel | LAT 48°43' LONG 123°26' |
| Fraser Point | LAT 49°01' LONG 123°42' | Saturna Island | LAT 48°47' LONG 123°09' |
| Fulford Harbour | LAT 48°46' LONG 123°26' | Scott Island | LAT 48°58' LONG 123°42' |
| Gabriola Island | LAT 49°10' LONG 123°48' | Separation Point | LAT 48°44' LONG 123°34' |
| Gabriola Passage | LAT 49°08' LONG 123°43' | Sharpe Point | LAT 49°21' LONG 123°16' |
| Ganges | LAT 48°51' LONG 123°30' | Sherard Point | LAT 48°52' LONG 123°37' |
| Genoa Bay | LAT 48°46' LONG 123°36' | Sidney | LAT 48°39' LONG 123°24' |
| Georgina Point | LAT 48°52' LONG 123°17' | Stuart Channel | LAT 49°00' LONG 123°42' |
| Georgina Shoals | LAT 48°52' LONG 123°17' | Telegraph Harbour | LAT 48°58' LONG 123°40' |
| Gossip Island | LAT 48°53' LONG 123°19' | Tent Island | LAT 48°56' LONG 123°38' |
| Gossip Shoals | LAT 48°53' LONG 123°18' | Thetis Island | LAT 49°00' LONG 123°41' |
| Grave Point | LAT 48°51' LONG 123°35' | Thrasher Rock | LAT 49°09' LONG 123°39' |
| Helen Point | LAT 48°51' LONG 123°21' | Trincomali Channel | LAT 48°58' LONG 123°35' |
| Holland Bank | LAT 48°59' LONG 123°48' | Tumbo Reef | LAT 48°48' LONG 123°03' |
| Hospital Point | LAT 48°56' LONG 123°43' | Valdes Island | LAT 49°05' LONG 123°40' |
| Hospital Rock | LAT 48°56' LONG 123°43' | Vesuvius Bay | LAT 48°53' LONG 123°34' |
| Houstoun Passage | LAT 48°56' LONG 123°36' | Village Bay | LAT 48°51' LONG 123°19' |
| Hudson Island | LAT 48°58' LONG 123°41' | Whaler Bay | LAT 48°53' LONG 123°20' |
| Josling Point | LAT 48°56' LONG 123°38' | Yellow Point | LAT 49°02' LONG 123°45'' |
| Kulleet Bay | LAT 49°01' LONG 123°46' | | |

Early morning off the Sidney waterfront.

## Our Information Sources

Tom Davis, manufacturer, teaser lures
by Rhys Davis Ltd.

## For visitor information:

SAANICH PENINSULA VISITOR INFO
CENTRE
Box 2014
Sidney, BC V8L 3S3
Tel: (604) 656-0525
Fax: (604) 656-7102

# Sidney

To many people travelling by ferry between the Lower Mainland and Southern Vancouver Island, Sidney is simply a name on a green sign about 5 km south of the Swartz Bay terminal. Those with salmon fishing on their minds usually continue southward toward Victoria, Sooke and Port Renfrew or swing north toward one of Vancouver Island's many other popular saltwater fishing destinations. This is fine with most of the local anglers as they are rather used to the relatively uncrowded fishing conditions around their island-studded end of the Saanich Peninsula.

Those who do take the turnoff to Sidney will find a pleasant, picturesque seaside city of 11,000 that offers a full range of services and amenities. Like neighbouring Victoria and Sooke, the area waters provide dependable year-round chinook fishing and halibut fishing is never far off.

Although there are several marinas in the area, launch ramps are at a premium. Van Isle Marina at 2320 Harbour Road has a launch ramp and guest moorage, and the Sidney Anglers' Association has a well-maintained, double-wide concrete ramp at Tulista Park near the Anacortes ferry dock. There is ample parking and the launch fee is reasonable.

## Weather and Water Conditions

Tom Davis, owner of Rhys Davis Ltd., was born and raised in the Sidney area. Although he now lives near Sooke, he fished out of Sidney for over 40 years and knows its ocean waters intimately. After all, there is no better way to update and test his popular line of Rhys Davis teaser lures than to go out and use them, which means fishing all year round, weather permitting. According to Davis, many locals feel that winter provides the nicest fishery here as water conditions are generally calmer than during warmer weather. Prevailing winter winds are northeasters with occasional southeasters—either of which can rapidly turn stormy—so it always pays to keep a good weather watch. Springtime westerlies can also cause problems at times. Summertime patterns are typical West Coast—usually calm during the mornings followed by midday winds that make it uncomfortably bumpy. Prevailing summer westerlies are usually manageable but southeasters often turn nasty. As these winds usually fall off by 6 p.m., it is often possible to get back on the water for the evening bite.

While cruising these waters is relatively safe, prior to dropping your cannonballs it pays to study the applicable marine chart as this area is riddled with reefs and rocks and the bottom can rise from 42 to 9 metres in a matter of seconds. Once your gear is down, closely monitor the depth sounder to avoid hangups. Also stay aware of how tidal currents are affecting your trolling patterns. Unlike open water areas where floods and ebbs are rather uneventful, water flowing between and around these islands, rocks and reefs gets quite swift, and as the currents wander all over, anglers are often caught unaware by side-drifts into shallow water, resulting in lost gear. While not life-threatening, it can be hard on the bank account.

Fog is seldom a consistent problem, but it can happen at almost any time from August until mid-autumn. If your boat lacks a compass or Global Positioning System, don't even consider going out when fog is forecast.

It pays to monitor the depth sounder as some shoals rise up rapidly.

## Run Timing

In the Sidney area there is a general slow-down of salmon fishing from mid-September through October as migratory chinooks, pinks and sockeye have ascended the rivers. Otherwise, these waters offer fairly dependable fishing. Feeder chinooks to 10 pounds usually appear about early November.

May finds much larger early-run spawners mixed in with the feeder chinooks, and some of the year's largest fish are caught during this month. Throughout July and August you will continue encountering feeder chinooks but fall-run adults will also start showing up. July should also herald the appearance of sockeye and pink salmon but the run sizes fluctuate from year to year. Although some coho also appear, their numbers are quite small and fishing for them is not permitted due to conservation concerns.

A few large chinooks bound for the Fraser and local rivers remain in the area until mid-September, which is also when a few of the first new batch of small winter chinooks start appearing. However, as there are concerns for the health of lower Strait of Georgia chinook stocks, it is advisable to keep current with any spot closures or regulation changes that might come into effect on short notice. Tackle shops and marinas are usually up on this information or you can check on the DFO web site. Tom Davis points out that the Sidney Anglers Association established a chinook net pen-rearing program in 2003, which has resulted in returns showing up in the Sidney Channel and Saanichton Spit area each September.

## Hotspots and Tactics

Most of the feeder chinook fishery throughout the winter is concentrated around Coal Island, Moresby Island from Point Fairfax to Seymour Point, Sidney Channel and Hamley Point, though during the October slow season most of these are shakers. Other areas worth checking out include Dock Island, Imrie Island, Colburne Passage, Shute Pass from Knapp Island to Shute Rock, Miners Channel between Sidney Spit and Forrest Island, Cordova Channel, the Red Can Buoy at the north end of Sidney Channel and Wain Rock in Saanich Inlet.

Downrigging deep—within 10 feet of the bottom—is the standard winter tactic with fishing conducted out in the mid-channels, especially along steep drop-offs into deeper water or over deep flats. Herring and needlefish are the main winter forage, so bait preferences lean toward herring strip and small anchovies. Tom Davis recommends a Tiny Teaser with herring strip and an Anchovy Special with anchovies, either of them in green, glow green or any of the chrome series with green in them. Trail them 42 to 60 inches behind a Hot Spot or O'Ki flasher. He says that green and chartreuse are key colours in most Sidney area waters, and this is reflected in the hoochies and spoons that anglers generally turn to when bait isn't working.

Davis suggests that, when using hoochies during the summer, leader lengths should be adjusted to 24 to 32 inches for sockeye, a bit longer for pinks, but stick with 42 to 60 inches for chinooks. It pays to experiment so troll as many lines as feasible and vary the leader lengths until

This prize chinook was tempted by an army truck hoochie.

you determine which one turns on the salmon. He added that the most notable trend in recent years has been the surge in popularity of spoons, especially Luhr Jensen's Coyote spoons in green/chartreuse and glow.

This basic fishing pattern continues until February, but when adult herring appear on their spawning migration, consider larger lures and baits. Toward the tag end of April some early spring-run spawners in the 15- to 20-pound class should join the over-wintering chinooks. Downrigging close to the bottom remains the preferred tactic, but shallow gear used at first light will now start producing a few fish. By month's end when needlefish become the main forage, it's time to switch to small anchovies, slender herring strips in Tiny Teasers and needlefish-shaped drift-jigs.

For feeder chinooks off Coal Island, try downrigging from Shag Rock (east of the white marker off Killer Whale Point) to Dock Island then north to Charmer Point. During November and December, chinooks to 10 pounds are available in Satellite Channel and off the southern end of Moresby Island. Make your troll pattern from Point Fairfax, northwest along Moresby to Seymour Point, then south across Prevost Passage to Imrie Island. Other areas to consider are Colburne Passage off Swartz Bay, Shute Pass from Knapp Island northwest past Piers Island to Shute Rock, the top end of Miners Channel between Sidney Spit and Forrest Island, Cordova Channel between Cordova Spit (known locally as Saanichton Spit) and James Island. Wain Rock off Moses Point at the head of Saanich Inlet might also be worth checking out, but while Arbutus Island produces a few, they tend to be smaller fish.

By February and March the Red Can Buoy at the top end of Sidney Channel is worth a look from time to time. A good troll pattern in April is from the tip of the lagoon spit on Sidney Island to the Red Can then across to the northern tip of James Island (known locally as Village Spit). The Powder Wharf on the southeast end of James Island also turns on in late April. Try from the Powder Wharf along the beach to the flats on the south end of James Island. Another late April hotspot is Cordova Spit from its tip over to the cable marker on the small lagoon spit at James Island.

During the ebb tides in early May try trolling southward from the dolphin at the end of Village Spit along the sandy beach or eastward in the deeper water along the top end of James Island. Good bets in late May are the Red Can Buoy, Mandarte Island, Point Fairfax, Cordova

Spit and Sidney Spit. Larger chinooks are usually found in fairly shallow water, so move out of the deep channels and start fishing close in along the beaches, especially during the early mornings and evenings in areas that have good concentrations of needlefish. Troll close to the bottom with slender herring strips, small anchovies or small lures. A flasher or dodger can be effective if the water clarity has been affected by an algae bloom.

By June the action moves away from Cordova Spit and James Island but increases around Sidney Spit, Coal Island, Mandarte Island and Point Fairfax. Drift-jigging usually starts improving about now, especially with slender lures like the Stingsilda, Point Wilson Dart, and Dungeness Stinger. Drift-jigging usually remains productive well into September.

530 Tomic plug

By July most of these areas offer larger chinooks, with two of the best bets being around Coal Island and Sidney Spit. If sockeye and pink salmon show up in any numbers, one of the most productive areas is off "Pender Bluffs" along the western side of North Pender Island between Wallace Point northwest to Mouat Point. The fishing pattern now reverts to deep trolling during midday and shallow trolling during the early mornings or late evenings. Continue using the same needlefish-imitating baits, lures and drift-jigs for feeder chinooks, but try plugs or a large Tyee strip or anchovy for the maturing adults. Pinks and sockeye favour small pink hoochies trolled slowly behind revolving flashers, usually in as straight a line as possible.

August and right through until early September continues

Tom Moss, the inventor of Tomic Plugs, and his son Wayne with a trophy chinook that fell for a Tomic Spoon.

much the same as in July, but there is a month-long closure at Coal Island so check the *Tidal Waters Sport Fishing Guide*. Best bets now are around Moresby Island, Sidney Spit, Arbutus Island and Wain Rock and off Coal Island after it reopens. The top end of Satellite Channel (Hatch Point to Cape Keppel) is closed from September 1 to 29, so check the regulations. In late September there might still be a few larger chinooks around Coal Island, Point Fairfax and Wain Rock.

## AVAILABLE MARINE CHARTS

3310 Gulf Islands—Victoria Harbour to Nanaimo Harbour
3440 Race Rocks to D'Arcy Island
3441 Haro Strait, Boundary Pass and Satellite Channel
3462 Juan de Fuca Strait to Strait of Georgia
3476 Approaches to Tsehum Harbour

### Marine Chart Coordinates:

| Place Names: | | Place Names: | |
|---|---|---|---|
| Arbutus Island | LAT 48°42′ LONG 123°26′ | North Pender Island | LAT 48°47′ LONG 123°17′ |
| Bedwell Harbour | LAT 48°45′ LONG 123°15′ | Piers Island | LAT 48°42′ LONG 123°25′ |
| Cape Keppel | LAT 48°43′ LONG 123°29′ | Point Fairfax | LAT 48°42′ LONG 123°18′ |
| Charmer Point | LAT 48°41′ LONG 123°21′ | Powder Wharf | LAT 48°36′ LONG 123°20′ |
| Coal Island | LAT 48°41′ LONG 123°22 | Prevost Passage | LAT 48°42′ LONG 123°19′ |
| Cod Reefs (North and South) | LAT 48°40′ LONG 123°18′ | "Red Can Buoy" | LAT 48°38′ LONG 123°21′ |
| Colburne Passage | LAT 48°42′ LONG 123°25′ | Saanich Inlet | LAT 48°37′ LONG 123°30′ |
| Cordova Channel | LAT 48°36′ LONG 123°22′ | Saanich Peninsula | LAT 48°37′ LONG 123°26′ |
| Cordova Spit (Saanichton Spit) | LAT 48°36′ LONG 123°22′ | Satellite Channel | LAT 48°43′ LONG 123°26′ |
| D'Arcy Shoals | LAT 48°34′ LONG 123°18′ | Separation Point | LAT 48°44′ LONG 123°34′ |
| Dock Island | LAT 48°40′ LONG 123°21′ | Seymour Point | LAT 48°43′ LONG 123°20′ |
| Forrest Island | LAT 48°40′ LONG 123°20′ | Shag Rock | LAT 48°41′ LONG 123°20′ |
| Halibut Island | LAT 48°37′ LONG 123°16′ | Shute Passage | LAT 48°43′ LONG 123°23′ |
| Hamley Point | LAT 48°36′ LONG 123°16′ | Shute Reef | LAT 48°43′ LONG 123°26′ |
| Hatch Point | LAT 48°42′ LONG 123°32′ | Sidney | LAT 48°39′ LONG 123°24′ |
| Imrie Island | LAT 48°42′ LONG 123°20′ | Sidney Channel | LAT 48°37′ LONG 123°20′ |
| James Island | LAT 48°36′ LONG 123°21′ | Sidney Island | LAT 48°37′ LONG 123°18′ |
| Killer Whale Point | LAT 48°41′ LONG 123°23′ | Sidney Spit | LAT 48°39′ LONG 123°20′ |
| Knapp Island | LAT 48°42′ LONG 123°24′ | South Pender Island | LAT 48°45′ LONG 123°13′ |
| Mandarte Island | LAT 48°38′ LONG 123°17′ | Swanson Channel | LAT 48°46′ LONG 123°19′ |
| Miners Channel | LAT 48°38′ LONG 123°17′ | Swartz Bay | LAT 48°41′ LONG 123°24′ |
| Moresby Island | LAT 48°43′ LONG 123°19′ | Tulista Park | LAT 48°37′ LONG 123°23′ |
| Moses Point | LAT 48°41′ LONG 123°29′ | Wain Rock | LAT 48°41′ LONG 123°29′ |
| Mouat Point | LAT 48°47′ LONG 123°19′ | Wallace Point | LAT 48°44′ LONG 123°14′ |

# ABOUT THE AUTHORS

## Bob Jones

Although born and raised in southern
British Columbia, I didn't catch my first
salmon until 1958, which was when the
Royal Canadian Air Force saw fit to post
me to Comox on the central east coast of
Vancouver Island. That first fish was a
pink salmon, which at the time were not
held in very high esteem either as sport
fish or on the table. It was caught with
the trout-weight spinning outfit I had

used in the north Okanagan and Cariboo in the days when I worked
there as a logger prior to my enlistment in 1953 in the 1st Regiment
Royal Canadian Horse Artillery (in which I served for three years in "A"
Battery as a driver/operator). I thought that fish fought quite well,
thank you, and that evening my young bride, Vera, pan-fried it to per-
fection. Ever since then we have been enjoying pink salmon—catching
and eating them—whenever the opportunity has presented itself. Vera
and I enjoyed over nine years at RCAF Station Comox before my work
as a weapons technician (air) took us on two tours to RCAF 4 Wing,
Baden Soellingen, Germany, and two to Ontario: Canadian Forces Base
Uplands in Ottawa and CFB Borden, near Barrie. In 1980 after 27 years
of service, while stationed at CFB Esquimalt near Victoria, I took an
early release in order to pursue a career in writing, and the Comox
Valley seemed like the most logical place to settle. We have never
regretted it.

## Larry E. Stefanyk

I grew up fishing for Alberta's rainbow trout and pike, which prepared me for my first saltwater salmon experience while visiting Sooke. I landed two chinooks in the mid-teens, and the feeling of excitement that they generated never really left me. As a result, when I moved to Vancouver Island in 1988, I wasted no time in making the transition to saltwater fishing, which started a never-ending search for further knowledge about its marvelous denizens. With the purchase of my first boat, a 17-foot Double Eagle, I headed for Schooner Cove to try fishing on my own. It was truly a steep learning curve, but I read everything available and listened appreciatively to anyone who offered to help me with the how-to and where-to of saltwater fishing. While I was successful, my learning curve still continues to this day.

I have worked in the outdoor publishing industry since 1990 and I have published *Island Fisherman* magazine since 2000. This has provided opportunities to fish with some of the best guides on the coast, and the information they have shared with me is a constant source of wonder. I share many of my mentors' tactics and tips in *Island Salmon Fisherman*, plus a few of my own developed over the years.

# INDEX

Printed in Great Britain
by Amazon

36937522R00057